Learning JavaScript Fast: Essential Coding Skills for Beginners

Build Web Interactivity Using Powerful JavaScript Tools

Felix Lancaster

Table of Contents

INTRODUCTION

For individuals who want to rapidly and efficiently understand the foundations of JavaScript, "Learning JavaScript Fast: Essential Coding Skills for Beginners: Build Web Interactivity Using Powerful JavaScript Tools" is the perfect resource. This book, intended for novices, offers a methodical way to comprehend JavaScript, one of the most popular programming languages for web development. This book makes complicated ideas easy to understand and guarantees a seamless learning process, regardless of your level of programming experience.

JavaScript is one of the main technologies underlying dynamic apps, responsive user interfaces, and interactive websites. Gaining proficiency in it helps lay the groundwork for more complex programming abilities and offers opportunities for web development. This book emphasizes fundamental coding methods and offers concise explanations, useful examples, and detailed instructions. By following the lessons, Readers will learn about writing JavaScript code, working with site elements, and developing interactive features that improve user engagement.

This book's practical approach, which encourages readers to practice coding as they advance, is one of its strongest points. The content is organized to promote progressive learning rather than overloading students with extraneous details. Exercises and real-world applications guarantee that ideas are understood and used successfully. This book helps novices create useful web apps with JavaScript's robust features, emphasizing efficiency and simplicity.

The book also presents important JavaScript technologies that increase coding efficiency and expedite development.

Readers will build confidence in their programming skills as they get familiar with fundamental concepts, including functions, loops, and event handling. The main focus is writing clear, efficient code that can be applied to web projects.

Readers will have learned the fundamentals of JavaScript by the end of this book, allowing them to develop interactive websites and applications. This book is a good place to start for anyone wanting to learn more about technology or become a web developer. "Learning JavaScript Fast" makes learning JavaScript attainable for any novice with its concise explanations and useful examples.

CHAPTER I

JavaScript Fundamentals

Understanding JavaScript

JavaScript is essential to contemporary web development, one of the most popular programming languages worldwide. It is an interpreted, dynamic, high-level language that lets programmers make responsive and interactive web apps. Brendan Eich created JavaScript in 1995 while he was employed at Netscape. Since then, it has grown into a strong and adaptable language that can be used for both front-end and back-end development. Together with HTML and CSS, it is a fundamental technology that forms the foundation of web development. Because JavaScript can work with the Document Object Model (DOM), developers can make dynamic web pages that react to user interaction.

JavaScript's client-side execution is one of its primary characteristics; it minimizes the frequency of server calls, improving user experience and performance. JavaScript may operate directly within a web browser, enabling real-time changes and interactions without requiring a page reload, unlike traditional programming languages that mostly rely on server-side processing. This feature is especially helpful for contemporary web applications that need real-time updates, including social media sites, chat programs, and online gaming.

Although it uses a prototype-based architecture instead of the traditional class-based approach used by languages like Java and C++, JavaScript is an object-oriented programming language. JavaScript is a very flexible and adaptive language since its objects are dynamic and can inherit properties from other objects through prototypes. Without a strict class structure, developers may easily extend functionalities and write reusable code with this prototype-based inheritance approach.

Programming paradigms supported by the language include procedural, object-oriented, and functional. Because of this versatility, developers can select the best strategy for a particular task. Developers may write more succinct and manageable code thanks to JavaScript's functional programming features, which include closures, higher-order functions, and first-class functions. JavaScript's treatment of functions as first-class citizens makes it possible to use sophisticated strategies like callbacks and function composition, which are crucial for managing asynchronous actions.

JavaScript's asynchronous programming is essential, especially for web applications. Because JavaScript uses the event-driven programming paradigm, it can manage several jobs at once without causing the main execution thread to stall. Mechanisms like async/await, promises, and callbacks are used. Callbacks are functions run when a specific operation is finished and are supplied as parameters to other functions. Overusing callbacks, however, can result in "callback hell," which makes the code hard to read and maintain. To solve this problem, promises were established, offering a more organized method of managing asynchronous processes. They enable developers to handle mistakes when chaining several asynchronous operations effectively. By making asynchronous code appear and operate like synchronous code, the async/await syntax, added in ECMAScript 2017, makes asynchronous code even easier to read and manage.

The advent of ECMAScript (ES) standards, which specify the language's requirements, has had a major impact on JavaScript's development. 2009 saw the release of ECMAScript 5 (ES5), which included enhanced array techniques, JSON compatibility, and more stringent error handling. With its introduction of features like let and const for variable declarations, arrow functions, template literals, destructuring assignments, and the class syntax, ECMAScript 6 (ES6), published in 2015, represented a significant milestone. JavaScript's capabilities have been further enhanced and expanded in later releases, making it more effective and developer-friendly.

JavaScript libraries and frameworks have greatly influenced contemporary web development. Well-known front-end frameworks like Vue.js, Angular, and React offer organized methods for creating dynamic user interfaces. Facebook created React, which enables developers to create reusable user interface elements and optimizes rendering efficiency by using a virtual document object model. Google maintains the comprehensive framework Angular, which features a modular architecture, dependency injection, and two-way data binding. Known for its simplicity and adaptability, Vue.js has become more well-liked due to its lightweight design and ease of integration.

With the introduction of Node.js, JavaScript has also advanced significantly on the back end. With the help of the runtime environment Node.js, developers may create scalable and fast apps by allowing JavaScript to operate on the server side. Because it uses JavaScript's non-blocking, event-driven architecture, it is ideal for managing concurrent connections and real-time applications. A well-liked framework based on Node.js, Express.js offers a flexible and basic approach that makes developing web servers and APIs easier.

Beyond web development, JavaScript is used in various fields, including artificial intelligence, game development, and mobile application development. Developers can now use JavaScript to create cross-platform mobile applications, eliminating the need for distinct codebases for iOS and Android, thanks to frameworks like React Native. With libraries like Phaser and Three.js, which make creating 2D and 3D games easier, respectively, JavaScript has also found use in the game development industry. Furthermore, machine learning frameworks like TensorFlow.js are part of JavaScript's expanding ecosystem, allowing programmers to create AI-powered apps within the browser.

When using JavaScript, security must be taken into account. JavaScript is vulnerable to several security flaws, such as injection attacks, cross-site scripting (XSS), and cross-site request forgery (CSRF), because it runs mostly on the client side. Developers must adhere to best practices, including input validation, content security policies, and secure authentication techniques, to reduce these risks. Malicious scripts cannot run in the browser if user inputs are handled correctly and potentially dangerous characters are escaped.

JavaScript's performance has greatly improved with the development of JavaScript engines like Microsoft's Chakra, Mozilla's SpiderMonkey, and Google's V8.

JavaScript is a competitive option even for applications that require high performance since these engines use just-in-time (JIT) compilation techniques to maximize execution speed. Further enhancing JavaScript's capabilities is WebAssembly (Wasm), a supplementary technology that enables programmers to execute high-performance code written in languages like C and Rust inside the browser.

The JavaScript development environment has changed with the advent of strong tools and editors. Rich features like syntax highlighting, debugging support, and extensions specifically designed for JavaScript programming are offered by Integrated programming Environments (IDEs) like Visual Studio Code, WebStorm, and Sublime Text. Package managers like npm (Node Package Manager) and yarn make dependency management easier, while version control systems like Git let developers collaborate. Developers may rapidly examine and troubleshoot their code with the help of debugging tools like Chrome DevTools.

Testing is a crucial component of JavaScript development, which guarantees that programs operate effectively and accurately. Several testing frameworks, including Jest, Mocha, and Jasmine, offer strong solutions for unit testing, integration testing, and end-to-end testing. Automated testing enhances the quality and maintainability of code by spotting any problems early in the development process. Continuous integration and deployment (CI/CD) pipelines further optimize the development workflow by automating testing and deployment procedures.

With a huge ecosystem of open-source projects, libraries, and developer resources, the JavaScript community is thriving and always changing. Developers can learn, share, and work together on JavaScript projects using platforms like Stack Overflow, MDN Web Docs, and

GitHub, which are excellent knowledge bases. Developers can keep up with the most recent developments and trends in the JavaScript ecosystem by attending conferences like JSConf, React Summit, and Google I/O.

JavaScript has many benefits and is widely used, yet it also has drawbacks and critiques. Its lax typing, which can result in unexpected behavior and runtime errors, is one of the main issues. This problem is addressed by TypeScript, a Microsoft superset of JavaScript that introduces static typing, improves code quality, and increases developer efficiency. Furthermore, the asynchronous nature of JavaScript can occasionally make controlling state and data flow more difficult, necessitating careful architecture choices and design patterns.

It is anticipated that JavaScript will continue to develop due to developer needs and continuous improvements in web technologies. Future JavaScript development will probably be influenced by the emergence of WebAssembly, progressive web apps (PWAs), and serverless computing. JavaScript will continue to dominate the programming scene with ongoing enhancements to developer experience, security, and performance.

To sum up, JavaScript is a strong and adaptable language that has transformed web development and expanded its use across various technological fields. It is an essential tool for developers everywhere because of its dynamic nature, adaptability, and extensive ecosystem. Leveraging the language's full potential will require adopting new frameworks, standards, and best practices as it develops. Unquestionably, JavaScript has a significant impact and a bright future because it keeps spurring innovation in the rapidly evolving digital space.

JavaScript Basics

JavaScript is one of the most important programming languages in the contemporary digital world. Web development frequently uses it to create dynamic, responsive, and interactive web pages. A large percentage of the internet is powered by JavaScript, a powerful and adaptable language developed by Brendan Eich in 1995 while employed at Netscape. JavaScript, which facilitates user interaction and improves the overall browsing experience, is generally utilized in front-end web development, in contrast to other programming languages primarily used for back-end development.

JavaScript is an interpreted, high-level language that doesn't require compilation and runs immediately in web browsers. With support for functional, imperative, and object-oriented programming methods, this multi-paradigm language is incredibly flexible for many development requirements. ECMAScript is the standardized specification for JavaScript, which has changed significantly since its beginnings. Because of this standardization, developers can design code that functions flawlessly in various situations by ensuring uniformity across platforms and browsers.

The ability of JavaScript to work with the Document Object Model (DOM) is one of its core features. JavaScript enables developers to dynamically alter components, properties, and styles, whereas the DOM depicts an HTML document's structure as a tree of nodes. This feature makes creating interactive websites that react to user mouse movements, keystrokes, and clicks possible. There are several ways to select and work with elements in JavaScript, including `getElementById()`, `querySelector()`, and `getElementsByClassName()`. These techniques improve user experience by making it simpler to make real-time changes to web content.

In JavaScript, variables are declared using `var`, `let`, or `const` and are used to hold data. Originally used for variable declaration, the `var` keyword had scope problems, which is why ES6 introduced `let` and `const`. The `let` keyword is safer and more predictable than' var' because it permits the definition of block-scoped variables. Conversely, constants whose values cannot be changed are declared with the `const` keyword. Code dependability and maintainability have significantly increased due to this differentiation between `let` and `const`.

Numerous data kinds, including simple types like numbers, strings, booleans, `null`, `undefined`, and `symbol`, are supported by JavaScript. JavaScript also includes sophisticated data types like arrays and objects. Structured data is commonly stored in JavaScript objects, which are collections of key-value pairs. Arrays are unique object types that enable the organized storage of many values. Data manipulation is made more efficient by JavaScript's many built-in functions for manipulating arrays, such as `push()`, `pop()`, `shift()`, `unshift()`, `map()`, `filter()`, and `reduce()`.

An essential component of JavaScript, functions enable programmers to encapsulate reusable code blocks. The `function` keyword or arrow functions introduced in ES6 can be used to declare functions. By automatically binding `this` to their lexical scope and offering a more condensed syntax, arrow functions lessen frequent JavaScript context-related problems. The ability of functions to take parameters and return results makes it possible to write modular and maintainable code. Higher-order functions, or those that take other functions as arguments or return them as results, are also supported by JavaScript. Programming paradigms that use functional programming require this competence.

JavaScript control structures, such as loops and conditionals, allow programmers to manage how code is executed. Program decision-making is made possible by conditional statements such as `if`, `else if`, and `else`. Code is made more legible and efficient using the `switch` statement instead of numerous `if-else` clauses. Redundancy is decreased by loops, such as `for`, `while`, and `do-while`, which allow code blocks to be executed again. While `map()`, `filter()`, and `reduce()` offer functional ways to array processing, the ES6 feature `forEach()` streamlines array iteration.

Because JavaScript is an event-driven language, event listeners react to user input. JavaScript functions are triggered by events like clicks, mouse movements, keystrokes, and form submissions, allowing web pages to behave dynamically. By attaching event handlers to items using the `addEventListener()` method, developers may ensure that particular actions are carried out in response to an event. By enabling a parent element to manage events for several child elements, event delegation, a JavaScript method, reduces the number of event listeners required and enhances performance.

Asynchronous programming is essential in JavaScript, particularly when working with timers, file reading, and API requests. Callbacks had historically been used in JavaScript to manage asynchronous tasks. Still, they frequently resulted in "callback hell," which made code challenging to read and maintain by offering a more streamlined method of handling success and failure conditions. Promises, which were introduced in ES6, enhanced asynchronous handling. A promise is a value that could exist right now, in the future, or never at all. Code can be made more legible by chaining operations using the `.then()` and `.catch()` methods. With the addition of the `async` and `await` keywords in ES8, JavaScript significantly enhanced asynchronous programming by enabling programmers to write asynchronous code that seems synchronous, increasing readability and maintainability.

Additionally, JavaScript is essential to contemporary web development frameworks and libraries. In previous years, well-known tools like jQuery simplified DOM manipulation and event handling, but more recent frameworks like React, Angular, and Vue have raised the bar for JavaScript development. Facebook's React introduced the idea of a virtual DOM, which reduced the need for direct DOM manipulations and improved performance. Google's Angular offers a complete MVC framework for creating dynamic web apps. Because of its ease of use and adaptability, Vue.js has become increasingly popular among developers as a tool for quickly and easily designing dynamic user interfaces.

JavaScript's ability to communicate with external APIs, which permits dynamic data retrieval and integration, is another potent feature. JavaScript may interact with web servers through APIs like Axios and the Fetch API, which enable asynchronous data retrieval and transmission. The `XMLHttpRequest` method has been replaced with the Fetch API, which offers a straightforward approach for making HTTP calls. A key idea in JavaScript development, JSON (JavaScript Object Notation) is frequently used to transfer data between a client and a server.

JavaScript drives back-end apps via Node.js, so it's not just for client-side programming. With the help of the runtime environment Node.js, developers may create scalable server-side apps by enabling JavaScript to operate outside of the browser. Node.js is ideal for real-time applications like chat programs, online gaming, and live streaming services because of its event-driven, non-blocking I/O style, making it especially effective at managing several requests. The development process is made simpler by the extensive ecosystem of packages that Node.js offers through npm (Node Package Manager).

Because JavaScript is a language that is frequently used for web applications, security is a major concern. SQL injection, cross-site request forgery (CSRF), and cross-site scripting (XSS) are common security risks. To reduce security concerns, developers must follow best practices including input validation, escaping user-generated information, and putting information Security Policies (CSP) into place. Additionally, by ensuring encrypted connection between the client and server, HTTPS guards against illegal access and data interception.

Error correction and debugging are crucial components of JavaScript development. The browser console and DevTools, two built-in debugging tools in JavaScript, assist developers in finding and resolving problems quickly. While the `debugger` statement enables establishing breakpoints in the code, the `console.log()` function is frequently used for debugging. To prevent unforeseen failures from impairing the functionality of applications, JavaScript additionally provides error-handling techniques through `try`, `catch`, and `finally` blocks.

JavaScript's future is bright, with ECMAScript standards enabling constant updates and enhancements. JavaScript is now more capable and developer-friendly thanks to features like optional chaining, bullish coalescing, and WebAssembly improvements. With its increasing use in fields like artificial intelligence (AI), the Internet of Things (IoT), and progressive web applications (PWAs), JavaScript remains the industry standard for online development.

To sum up, JavaScript is an essential programming language that has revolutionized web application development and user experience. Both novice and seasoned developers favor it because of its adaptability, simplicity of use, and strong ecosystem. JavaScript has countless applications, from asynchronous programming and back-end development with Node.js to modifying the DOM and managing events. JavaScript keeps developing as technology does, guaranteeing its continued applicability in the dynamic field of web development. Anyone wishing to create cutting-edge, interactive, and effective web apps must understand JavaScript basics.

Control Flow and Loops

Programming fundamentals like control flow and loops determine the sequence in which statements are performed. Writing effective, well-structured, and maintainable code requires an understanding control flow and loops. While loops offer a way to run a block of code repeatedly depending on predetermined circumstances, control flow dictates the order in which instructions are executed within a program. These ideas are essential for automating tedious operations, addressing real-world software development issues, and enhancing programs' dynamic and interactive nature.

In programming, control flow describes the sequence in which certain words, instructions, or function calls are carried out or assessed. Programs, by default, carry out assertions one after the other, from top to bottom. On the other hand, programming languages include structures that let programmers change this flow by making choices, carrying out operations again, or switching between code sections in response to certain circumstances. Instead of running from beginning to end in a set way, these control structures give programs greater flexibility by enabling them to react dynamically to various inputs and events.

Because they allow programs to run distinct code blocks based on predetermined criteria, conditional statements are essential to control flow. Usually, these conditions are the foundation for comparisons or assessments of variables, user inputs, or other program states. By utilizing conditional logic, developers can design systems that respond intelligently to various scenarios. This is particularly helpful for applications that need to make decisions, such as financial transactions, form validation, game logic, and authentication systems. By guiding the program along several courses, conditional statements ensure that particular conditions dictate how the code runs.

Another crucial control flow component is loops, which let programmers run a code block repeatedly in response to a specified condition. Loops allow code to be run repeatedly rather than having repeating statements written by hand, increasing program efficiency and decreasing redundancy. Loops are employed in many applications, including automating repetitive processes, analyzing big datasets, and iterating over lists or arrays. Without having to create distinct instructions for every piece, they enable developers to work with data dynamically and execute operations on numerous elements.

When the number of repetitions is unknown beforehand or when specific requirements must be fulfilled before execution ends, loops are especially helpful. They enable handling complicated calculations, iterating over data sets, and carrying out repetitive activities until a certain result is obtained. Loops are frequently coupled with conditional statements to give greater control over how they are executed. This ensures the loop executes when required and ends when the intended outcome is achieved.

It is impossible to overestimate the significance of loops in programming. They serve as the foundation for numerous algorithms and data processing strategies, allowing programmers to manage vast volumes of data effectively. Without loops, programmers would have to write redundant code, which would lengthen programs, make them more difficult to maintain, and increase the likelihood of errors. Programmers can simplify and add dynamic elements to their systems by employing loops efficiently.

Loops are also essential for performance optimization. Using loops, computers can handle various tasks rapidly and efficiently instead of doing repetitive procedures by hand. Applications requiring data manipulation, such as sorting algorithms, mathematical computations, and artificial intelligence models, benefit greatly from this. Such calculations would be time-consuming and unfeasible without loops, particularly when working with big datasets.

One of its main benefits is that loops can be used with a variety of data structures. Iterating over lists, arrays, or objects is necessary for many applications to retrieve, alter, or analyze data. Loops make operating on these data structures simple, eliminating the need to retrieve each piece individually. Applications where massive volumes of data must be processed effectively, such as social networking platforms, inventory management systems, and search engines, require this.

Loops can be divided into many categories based on how they work and when they carry out their conditions. While some loops continue to run until a certain condition is met, others are made to run for a certain amount of iterations. Developers can select the best program strategy by knowing the distinctions between different loop types. Choosing the appropriate loop structure is crucial to ensuring that code executes quickly and avoids pointless calculations or endless loops, which can make systems crash or become unresponsive.

Writing effective code requires controlling loop execution. Loops that are not properly optimized might cause delayed program execution, high memory utilization, and performance problems. It's critical to ensure loops have well-stated exit conditions to avoid endless looping. When the terminating condition is never satisfied, the program runs indefinitely, known as an infinite loop. These issues can cause system crashes or unresponsive apps and be challenging to debug. Developers must carefully craft their loop conditions and ensure there is a clear path for the loop to exit to avoid such problems.

When working with multidimensional data structures in programming, nested loops—where one loop is nested inside another—are frequently utilized. These loops enable operations on intricate datasets, including processing matrices, tables, and grids. However, if nested loops are not correctly controlled, they can increase computational complexity and slow down code. Optimization strategies must be considered to improve performance when working with nested loops. To guarantee optimal speed, developers should try to reduce the number of iterations whenever feasible and steer clear of pointless calculations.

In addition to being utilized in simple programming tasks, loops and control flow are the cornerstone of more complex computer science ideas. They are crucial in game development, cryptography, artificial intelligence, and data science. For instance, loops are frequently used by machine learning algorithms to handle big datasets and train models. Loops are used in cybersecurity to examine encrypted communications and find trends in security flaws. Loops are used in gaming to dynamically handle user interactions, detect collisions, and control animations.

The effect loops have on the readability and maintainability of code is another crucial factor to consider. Although loops offer strong features, code with excessive or complex loop structures may be challenging to comprehend and debug. To make loop logic easier to read, describing it clearly and succinctly is crucial, using descriptive variable names and including comments as needed. It is simpler for other developers to comprehend and alter code when loops are kept simple and superfluous nesting is avoided.

Beyond conventional programming languages, loops and control flow patterns are frequently used in data analysis, automation, and web development. Loops are used by many online applications to manage user interactions, create material dynamically, and update user interfaces in real-time. Loops are used in automation scripts to carry out repetitive operations, including file manipulation, data extraction, and system monitoring. Loops are used by data analysts to efficiently process and analyze enormous datasets, extracting insightful information and producing reports.

As programming advances, new methods and best practices for working with loops and control flow structures emerge. To increase code efficiency, readability, and performance, developers always look for ways to optimize loops. The additional capabilities and tools offered by contemporary programming languages and frameworks make working with loops easier and more powerful. Keeping abreast of the most recent improvements in software engineering requires understanding these developments and the ability to use them effectively.

Loops and control flow are essential programming building blocks that let programmers make dynamic, responsive, and effective applications. Programmers can create more efficient and streamlined programs by comprehending how loops automate repetitive activities, and control flow determines how code is executed. It is crucial to grasp these ideas to create dependable and maintainable software, whether dealing with simple scripts or large-scale applications. The ability to use control flow and loops efficiently is still a crucial talent for developers in all areas of programming, even as technology advances.

Functions and Scope

Writing effective, legible, and maintainable code is based on two core programming concepts: functions and scope. To write modular, reusable, and well-structured code—which eventually results in more reliable and scalable applications—developers must understand these ideas. The visibility and lifetime of variables within a program are determined by scope, whereas functions enable developers to encapsulate code into self-contained blocks that carry out specified activities. Gaining proficiency in programming and creating high-caliber software requires understanding how functions and scope interact.

Fundamentally, a function is a code created to carry out a specific duty. Functions can be called from other code sections and are defined using a function declaration or expression. Functions can take parameters as input, process them, and then return the outcome. Functions are flexible and effective tools for managing and organizing code because of their capacity to receive input and produce output. Developers can write modular code that is simpler to comprehend, test, and maintain by decomposing complicated tasks into smaller, more manageable units. A well-structured program is made up of functions that encourage code reuse and cut down on redundancy.

Code reuse is one of the functions' main advantages. With functions, programmers may create code once and use it again throughout the application. Because the same logic isn't repeated in several locations, this lessens duplication and the likelihood of mistakes. Take software that must determine the average of a range of values, for instance. The developer can write a function that accepts an array as input, computes the average, and returns the result rather than writing the same logic repeatedly. To ensure consistency and lower the possibility of errors, this function can be used every time the average is computed. Code bases become more efficient and maintainable when functions are used to reuse code.

Functions also encourage encapsulation and abstraction. By concealing a function's implementation specifics, abstraction enables the user to engage with the function via a clearly defined interface. Because the user does not need to comprehend the inner workings of the function, the code is made simpler and easier to grasp. Contrarily, encapsulation entails combining relevant data and code into a single unit, like a function, and limiting access to the internal specifics. This ensures the code's integrity is preserved and accidental disruption of the function's internal operations is avoided. Functions enhance the overall readability and maintainability of the code by encouraging abstraction and encapsulation.

Functions' capacity to enhance code readability and organization is another crucial feature. By segmenting it into smaller, independent parts, developers can produce software with a clear, logical structure that is simpler to use and comprehend. It can be easier to find and change code when necessary if each function is made to carry out a specified duty. This modular approach makes communication easier because various team members may work on distinct tasks without interfering with each other's code. To further improve code readability and maintainability, functions can be documented with comments describing their parameters, return values, and purpose. Easy maintenance and long-term project success depend on well-structured code.

Functions are crucial for managing complicated tasks and algorithms in addition to their significance in code organization and reuse. Writing and maintaining code in a single block is difficult; many real-world situations require complex logic and several stages to solve. These intricate activities can be divided into smaller, more manageable steps by developers using functions, each contained within a function. Take a sorting algorithm that must arrange a range of numbers, for instance. The developer can write distinct methods for operations like array partitioning, element comparison, and element swapping rather than coding the complete sorting algorithm in a single block. This facilitates testing and debugging of each function and makes the code easier to read. Functions offer an organized method for resolving challenging issues.

Conversely, scope establishes the variables' lifetime and visibility within a program. The scope of variables in programming establishes where they can be accessed and changed. To successfully manage variables and avoid disagreements and mistakes, it is essential to comprehend the scope. Global scope and local scope are the two primary categories of scope. Whereas variables declared in the local scope are only available within the function or block in which they are defined, variables declared in the global scope can be accessed from anywhere in the program. When scope is properly managed, variables are used appropriately and don't conflict.

"Global scope" describes a program's outermost scope, where variables are declared outside any blocks or functions. Anywhere in the application can access and change variables in the global scope since they have global visibility. Global variables present dangers like accidental changes and name conflicts, even though they might be useful for exchanging data across many software components. It is generally advised to employ local variables whenever possible and minimize the use of global variables to reduce these hazards. An excessive number of global variables might result in code that is hard to maintain and prone to mistakes.

Conversely, local scope describes the scope inside a block or function. Declared variables are only available inside the designated function or block; they cannot be accessed outside of it. This restricted visibility guards against unintentional interference from other software components and preserves the integrity of the variables. Local scope is especially crucial for functions because it enables programmers to write independent code segments with their variables and states. This encapsulation makes the code more dependable and manageable by preventing variables inside a function from conflicting with variables in other program sections. A clean and well-organized code structure is maintained with the aid of local variables.

Block scope, which describes the scope inside a particular block of code, like a loop or conditional statement, is supported by certain programming languages in addition to global and local scope. Because block scope enables developers to restrict the visibility of variables to the exact block where they are required, it is especially helpful for handling variables within loops and conditional statements. This guarantees that variables are only available when pertinent and helps avoid name conflicts. Writing simple and concise code requires understanding block scope, particularly in languages that enable this feature.

Since a variable's scope is frequently dictated by the function or block in which it is declared, functions and scope are closely connected ideas. Effective variable management and avoiding common issues like variable shadowing and hoisting require understanding how scope operates within functions. When a local variable in a block or function has the same name as a variable in the outer scope, this is known as variable shadowing. In these situations, the outside variable becomes unreachable within the function or block since the local variable "shadows" it. If not handled appropriately, this may result in unexpected behavior and issues. Developers should know the variable scope and use descriptive and unambiguous names to prevent variable shadowing.

Another crucial idea about scope, especially in JavaScript, is hoisting. During the execution phase, variable and function declarations are shifted to the top of their containing scope, a process known as hoisting. This implies that functions and variables can be utilized before their declaration in the code. Although hoisting has many uses, if it is not fully understood, it can also cause confusion and unexpected behavior. Declaring variables and functions near the start of their respective scopes is generally advised to prevent hoisting-related problems. Writing consistent and error-free code requires an understanding of hoisting.

Writing effective and maintainable code requires a careful balance between functions and scope. Developers can produce modular, reusable code that is simpler to comprehend and maintain by using functions to structure and encapsulate functionality. By ensuring that variables are only available when they are required, proper scope management lowers the possibility of errors and conflicts. Functions and scope work together to create organized programming, which empowers programmers to create intricate and reliable programs. Writing excellent code and developing scalable software solutions require adherence to these guidelines.

Functional programming, a programming paradigm that avoids modifying state or changeable data and views computing as executing mathematical functions, relies heavily on functions. Functions are first-class citizens in functional programming, which means they can be assigned to variables, returned as values from other functions, and supplied as arguments to different functions. Higher-order functions—those that accept other functions as arguments or return them as results—are made possible by this. Functional programming is an effective technique for controlling complexity in software development because higher-order functions allow for strong abstractions and code reuse.

Pure functions, which always yield the same result given the same input and have no side effects, are emphasized in functional programming languages like Haskell, Lisp, and Scala. Since pure functions don't rely on or change the program's state, they are simpler to test and understand. Because pure functions can be run separately without race conditions or state inconsistencies, functional programming is ideally suited for parallel and concurrent programming. Developers can produce more predictable and maintainable code by comprehending the fundamentals of functional programming and the function's place in this paradigm.

In object-oriented programming (OOP), a programming paradigm that centers software design around objects—instances of classes—scope is also essential. Scope in OOP aids in defining the accessibility and visibility of methods and attributes inside classes and objects. Class-based scope aids in encapsulation by deciding which class members are reachable from other program areas. A key tenet of object-oriented programming (OOP) is encapsulation, which entails exposing only a clearly defined interface while concealing an object's internal state and implementation specifics. This encourages modular and maintainable programming while safeguarding the object's integrity.

Access modifiers like public, private, and protected are used in OOP to manage class members' visibility. Private members can only be reached within the class, but public members can be reached anywhere in the software. Within the class and its subclasses, protected members can be accessed. By employing access modifiers, developers can enforce encapsulation and ensure that an object's internal state isn't accidentally exposed or changed. Writing reliable and safe object-oriented code requires careful scope and access modifiers handling.

CHAPTER II

Working with Data in JavaScript

Understanding Data Structures

As the foundation of effective data storage, retrieval, and manipulation, data structures are essential to computer science and programming. A data structure is a specific method for managing, arranging, and storing data that makes access and changes easier. Developers must comprehend the qualities, benefits, and use cases of data structures since they directly impact how well algorithms and applications work. Databases, artificial intelligence, networking, operating systems, and software development are just a few fields that use data structures. They are essential for increasing the effectiveness of problem-solving procedures and optimizing computing activities.

Studying data structures aims to comprehend the effective storage and retrieval of various kinds of data. Data structures can be divided into two primary categories: linear and nonlinear. Thanks to linear data structures, access is possible in a linear order, which preserves the elements' sequential ordering. Arrays, linked lists, stacks, and queues are typical examples. Conversely, nonlinear data structures allow for more intricate interactions between parts by organizing data hierarchically or linked. Graphs, hash tables, and trees are a few types of nonlinear structures. Several variables, including memory limitations, data access patterns, and computational complexity, influence the best data structure type for a given application.

One of the simplest and most used data structures is an array, which comprises a group of elements kept at consecutive memory regions. They make retrieval procedures more efficient by enabling direct access to aspects through an index. Nevertheless, arrays have finite sizes, which may result in memory wastage if they are not used to their full potential or necessitate resizing if they are. Linked lists, on the other hand, offer a dynamic substitute in which items are kept in nodes linked by pointers. Because linked lists don't need to allocate memory contiguously as arrays do, insertions and deletions can be done quickly. However, their disadvantage is the extra memory expense needed to store pointers and the requirement for sequential traversal to access elements.

Specialized linear data structures like stacks and queues use certain rules to access items. The most recent piece added to a stack is the first to be removed, according to the Last In, First Out (LIFO) concept. Applications like function call management, expression evaluation, and backtracking algorithms frequently employ this structure. On the other hand, the First In, First Out (FIFO) concept guarantees that elements be processed in the order in which they were added to a queue. Task scheduling, web server request processing, and operating system process management depend on queues. The functionality of basic queues is extended by variants, including circular queues, priority queues, and double-ended queues, which offer more flexibility for certain applications.

One root node acts as the starting point for trees, which are hierarchical data structures of nodes connected by edges. A branching structure can be formed by each node having several child nodes. Applications like file systems, search engines, and database indexing frequently use trees. Many specialized tree topologies are based on binary trees, where each node has a maximum of two offspring. By guaranteeing that each left child has a value lower than its parent and each right child has a value higher than its parent, binary search trees (BSTs) offer an effective method of storing and retrieving sorted data. This characteristic makes logarithmic time complexity for search, insertion, and deletion operations possible. AVL trees and Red-Black trees are examples of self-balancing trees that use rotation operations to maintain a balanced structure because imbalanced BSTs might impair performance.

Another tree variant created especially for priority-based applications is heaps. A complete binary tree in which the parent node upholds a particular order relationship with its offspring is called a heap. The parent node in a min-heap has the smallest value, whereas the parent node in a max-heap has the biggest value. Priority queues, sorting algorithms like Heap Sort, and graph algorithms like Dijkstra's shortest path are the main applications for heaps. The ability of heaps to preserve the heap property during insertions and deletions, which guarantees the ideal time complexity for priority-based operations, is what gives them their efficiency.

Graphs are flexible data structures that show relationships between entities by connecting nodes (vertices) with edges. There are two sorts of graphs: directed and undirected. Directed graphs have edges that point in certain directions, whereas undirected graphs have edges that point in both directions. Applications like recommendation engines, computer networks, social networks, and transportation systems substantially use graphs. They serve as the basis for several algorithms, such as the Dijkstra algorithm for determining the shortest path, the Kruskal and Prim algorithms for creating minimal spanning trees, and the breadth-first search (BFS) and depth-first search (DFS) algorithms for traversing graphs. Depending on how many connections there are between nodes, the adjacency list and adjacency matrix—two popular graph representations—have different benefits.

Using key-value pairs, hash tables—also called hash maps—offer an effective method of storing and retrieving data. They provide direct access to elements by computing an index using a hashing technique. Associative arrays, caching systems, and database indexing all use hash tables extensively. The average constant time complexity of hash tables for lookups, deletions, and insertions is a significant benefit. However, collisions may happen when several keys map to the same index, necessitating conflict-resolution strategies like chaining or open addressing. Choosing the right hashing algorithm reduces collisions and guarantees effective operation.

The particular needs of an issue, such as the frequency of operations, memory limitations, and access patterns, determine which data structure is best. For instance, linked lists might be better than arrays if frequent insertions and deletions are required because linked lists are dynamic. A binary search tree or hash table might be more appropriate if quick lookups are a top concern. Trees are superior to hash tables, which do not preserve order when ordered traversal is necessary. The worst-case, average-case, and best-case scenarios of operations are expressed using Big O notation, which is frequently used to assess the efficiency of data structures based on time and space complexity.

Data structure implementation is essential in practical applications, such as software development and scientific computing. B-trees and B+ trees are used in database management systems to index big datasets, facilitating quick search and retrieval processes. File systems enable hierarchical file and directory organization through directory topologies that resemble trees. Routing algorithms in networking use graph topologies to identify the best routes for sending data. Game trees in chess engines and knowledge graphs in semantic search systems are two examples of artificial intelligence applications that use trees and graphs to make decisions.

Data structures are essential to two basic operations: sorting and searching. Different techniques are used by sorting algorithms, including Bubble Sort, Quick Sort, and Merge Sort, to arrange elements in a predetermined order. Recursively splitting big datasets into smaller subarrays and then recombining them in sorted order is how Merge Sort, which is based on the divide-and-conquer strategy, effectively sorts them. Another divide-and-conquer method, Quick Sort, divides the array into smaller and larger elements after choosing a pivot element. It then sorts each split recursively. Despite its simplicity, bubble Sort's quadratic time complexity makes it ineffective for huge datasets. Algorithms for searching, such as binary and linear search, identify whether an element is present in a dataset. The binary search uses an array's sorted order to do logarithmic-time searches, which greatly increases efficiency compared to linear search, which scans each element one after the other.

Technological developments have produced complex data structures that are tailored for particular uses. Persistent data structures make version control and undo actions possible, which permit changes without changing the original structure. In caching and security applications, bloom filters offer a probabilistic data structure for membership queries that is space-efficient. Fast string matching and prefix-based searches in text processing and dictionary applications are made possible by Tries, a specialized tree structure. Skip lists allow logarithmic-time search, insertion, and deletion operations and offer an alternative to balanced trees for preserving sorted data.

Continuous advancements are being made in studying data structures to maximize memory and performance. Managing data structures over numerous processors and nodes has become more difficult due to parallel and distributed computing, requiring concurrent access and synchronization methods. Data structures that can effectively handle large datasets have become more and more crucial as big data and artificial intelligence have grown in popularity. The importance of data structures in contemporary computing is demonstrated by machine learning and data analytics processing and analyzing massive amounts of data using optimal structures.

Any programmer or computer scientist must have a solid understanding of data structures since they are the cornerstone of effective algorithm design and software development. Developers can create scalable apps, maximize performance, and successfully tackle challenging issues with a solid understanding of data structures. The need for effective data structures will continue to be a crucial component of computational science as technology advances. Data structures will be essential in forming the digital world, whether in big data analytics, artificial intelligence, or traditional software engineering.

Manipulating Strings and Numbers

Programming requires the ability to manipulate strings and numbers for developers to process, analyze, and alter data efficiently. Most programming languages use strings and integers as basic data types, and working with them is essential for resolving various issues, from straightforward text processing to intricate numerical computations. Any programmer who wants to produce effective, reliable, and maintainable code must understand the different methods and functions available for working with strings and integers.

In programming, strings are collections of characters that stand in for textual data. They may include whitespace characters, symbols, numerals, and letters. There are several uses for strings, including handling text-based data, displaying messages, and saving user input. Developers frequently have to do operations like concatenation, slicing, searching, replacing, and formatting to work with strings. These operations allow programmers to change and examine strings in various ways, making them an effective text-processing tool.

Concatenation is the technique of connecting two or more strings to create a single string. This function is frequently used to build file paths, generate dynamic messages, and merge user input with prewritten text. The plus operator (+) or a specific concatenation function performs concatenation in most computer languages. For instance, the code below concatenates two strings in Python: result = str1 + " " + str2 str1 = "Hello" str2 = "World." The string "Hello World" is created by connecting str1 and str2 with a space between them. Concatenation is a common process in string manipulation, which is straightforward but effective.

Substring extraction, often called slicing, is extracting a string section using predetermined start and end indices. This function helps extract pertinent information from strings, including collecting certain user input segments, separating file extensions, and parsing date components. In Python, slicing is done by defining the range of indices with square brackets and a colon. For instance, to extract a substring from a given string, use the code below: "abcdef" is the text value. Substring = [1:4] text By providing the start index (1) and the finished index (4), this code extracts the substring "bcd" from the string "abcdef." Slicing offers a versatile method of accessing particular string segments.

Another popular string manipulation action is searching for substrings within a string. This entails detecting if a specific substring is included in the main string and, if yes, where it is located. This process is helpful for tasks like developing search capabilities, analyzing text data, and validating user input. To find a substring in Python, utilize the find method: location = text.find("World"), text = "Hello World." This code returns the beginning index of the substring (6) after searching for the substring "World" within the text "Hello World". The find method returns -1 if the substring cannot be located. Finding substrings is a basic text analysis and processing activity.

Another crucial step in string manipulation is swapping out substrings inside a string. This entails changing one substring for another, which is helpful for things like data sanitization, text formatting, and find-and-replace feature implementation. Substrings in Python can be changed using the replace method: new_text = text. replace text = "Hello World"("World," "Python") By substituting "World" for the substring "Python," this code creates the new string "Hello Python." Developers can modify text data to meet various needs by changing substrings.

A crucial step in producing dynamic and understandable text output is formatting strings. Variables and expressions are embedded into a string to create personalized messages, reports, and user interfaces. Most programming languages offer different ways to format strings, like JavaScript's template literals or Python's format function. The format method in Python can be applied as follows: message = "Name: {}, Age: {}" name = "Alice" age = 30.format(name, age) This code creates the formatted message "Name: Alice, Age: 30" by embedding the variables name and age within the string. Developers can produce dynamic, user-friendly text output by using string formatting.

Handling numbers is as vital for data analysis and numerical computations as manipulating strings is for text processing. In most programming languages, numbers are a basic data type used to represent quantities, measurements, and values. To work with numbers, developers must frequently perform mathematical functions, arithmetic computations, rounding, and type conversion. Thanks to these methods, developers can address various issues and efficiently process numerical data.

The simplest operations on numbers are arithmetic computations. These consist of modulus operations, addition, subtraction, multiplication, and division. Applications for arithmetic computations include data analysis, scientific simulations, and financial calculations. Arithmetic operations in most computer languages utilize conventional operators like +, -, *, /, and %. For instance, the following Python code performs simple arithmetic operations: Sum = a + b difference = a - b product = a * b quotient = a / b residual = a % b, a = 10 b = 3. The total, difference, product, quotient, and remainder of the numbers 10 and 3 are all determined by this code. Basic procedures that are necessary for numerical processing are arithmetic computations.

Another frequent procedure in numerical manipulation is rounding numbers. To do this, a number must be adjusted to the closest integer or a predetermined number of decimal places. Rounding is helpful for tasks like handling imperfect measurements, guaranteeing consistency in computations, and structuring numerical output. Numbers can be rounded in Python using the round function: value = 3.14159 rounded_value = round(value, 2). The value 3.14 is obtained by rounding 3.14159 to two decimal places using this code. Rounding offers a method for controlling numerical accuracy and displaying figures understandably.

Converting a value from one data type to another, like a string to an integer or the other way around, is known as type conversion. This activity depends on managing user input, carrying out computations, and combining various data sources. Typ conversion functions or methods are available in most programming languages to simplify this procedure. For instance, type conversion in Python can be accomplished using the int and float functions: integer_value = int(string_value) and string_value = "42" float_value(string_value) = float The text "42" is changed by this code into a floating-point number (42.0) and an integer (42). Values in the right format for the intended operations are guaranteed via type conversion.

Advanced numerical computations like exponentiation, logarithms, trigonometry, and statistics can be done using mathematical functions. Like Python's math module, standard libraries or modules frequently contain these functions. Developers can tackle intricate problems and carry out accurate computations thanks to mathematical functions. For instance, the math module in Python offers several mathematical functions: import math value = math.sqrt(value) = 16 square root logarithm = log(value) in math Using the math module, this code determines the integer 16's square root and natural logarithm. Scientific computing and numerical analysis need the use of mathematical functions.

Another aspect of handling numerical data is working with various numerical representations and formats, including complex, floating-point, and integer numbers. For efficient numerical manipulation, it is essential to comprehend each format's unique features and applications. Counting and indexing are two applications for integers: entire numbers devoid of decimal points. Measurements and continuous values are represented by floating-point numbers, which are real numbers with decimal points. Real and imaginary components make up complex numbers employed in sophisticated mathematical and engineering applications. Developers can handle numerical data and solve multiple challenges by comprehending and utilizing various numerical forms.

Controlling numerical accuracy and precision is a crucial component of number manipulation. Accuracy is the degree to which a computed value resembles the actual value, whereas numerical precision is the number of significant digits used to represent a number. Controlling accuracy and precision is essential to guaranteeing the dependability of numerical computations, particularly in financial and scientific applications. Potential problems such as rounding mistakes, floating-point imprecision, and numerical instability need to be understood by developers. Developers can guarantee precise numerical outputs and reduce errors using the right tools and procedures.

Apart from working with individual letters and integers, developers frequently have to deal with data sets like arrays, lists, and dictionaries. Thanks to these data structures, developers can efficiently store, arrange, and work with numerous strings and numbers. For instance, dictionaries hold key-value pairs, but arrays and lists offer a means to store elemental sequences. Developers may process and analyze massive datasets more easily using these data structures to carry out bulk operations like sorting, filtering, and aggregating data.

Sorting is a typical process of arranging data in a particular order, like descending or ascending. This procedure is helpful for tasks like showing sorted lists, looking for items, and monitoring trends. The sort function in Python is one of the built-in sorting functions or methods found in most computer languages: [5, 2, 9, 1, 5, 6] numbers are equal to numbers.sort() [1, 2, 5, 5, 6, 9] is the result of sorting the list of numbers using this code in ascending order. Developers can arrange data and carry out effective searches and analyses by sorting.

Filtering is choosing items from a collection according to predetermined standards. Tasks like cleaning databases, creating search capability, and extracting pertinent data can all benefit from this technique. Python filtering can be done using the filter function or list comprehensions: [5, 2, 9, 1, 5, 6] are the numbers. [num for num in numbers if num > 4] = filtered_numbers By filtering the list of numbers and choosing only those larger than 4, this code produces.

Handling Dates and Times

Managing dates and timings is essential to data analysis, system design, and programming. Numerous applications depend on precise timekeeping and data management to plan tasks, document occurrences, monitor durations, and synchronize data across several systems. Time zones, daylight saving time, leap years, and multiple calendar systems are some of the aspects that make working with dates and timings complicated. Building dependable software systems requires an understanding of how to handle these difficulties.

Knowing how dates and times are represented in computer systems is one of the most important parts of managing them. Timestamps, which indicate the number of seconds (or milliseconds) that have passed since a reference point, usually called the epoch, is used by most systems to store dates and times. The epoch in many contemporary computing environments and the Unix operating system is January 1, 1970, at 00:00:00 UTC. Calculations like comparing two dates or translating time between formats are easier when time is stored as a numerical value. But timestamps alone don't tell us about human-readable date formats, which differ by culture and location.

Through libraries and functions created to make common jobs easier, various programming languages offer built-in support for managing dates and times. For example, Python's `datetime` module can generate, modify, and format date and time objects. To address many facets of time representation, Java has the `java.time` package, which contains classes like `LocalDate`, `LocalTime`, and `ZonedDateTime`. While libraries like Moment.js and date-fns offer more capability, JavaScript's `Date` object lets programmers work with dates and times. Using these tools, developers may easily format dates, compute discrepancies, and convert across time zones.

Regarding dates and times, time zones add even another level of complexity. A time zone, typically defined as Coordinated Universal Time (UTC), is a region of the world that observes the same standard time. Applications that interact with users worldwide must consider time zone differences when storing and displaying time-related data because the Earth is divided into multiple time zones. To provide uniformity across many locales, timestamps are stored in UTC by many databases and operating systems. The system uses user settings or geographic data to determine the appropriate local time zone when displaying a date or time to users. In applications like online scheduling, financial transactions, and communication systems, where precise time representation guarantees that events transpire as anticipated across various regions, time zone conversion is especially important.

By adding recurring changes to standard time, daylight saving time (DST) makes time calculations even more difficult. To maximize daylight during specific months, many areas move their clocks backward in the fall and forward in the spring. Software systems that must adjust for the shifting time offsets face difficulties due to these modifications. Inaccurate scheduling, inaccurate time calculations, and inconsistent event logging can result from improper handling of daylight saving time. Modern programming frameworks frequently have built-in support for managing DST transitions to lessen these problems. Developers can work with time zones and automatically adapt to daylight-saving time changes with libraries like Java's `ZoneId` and Python's `pytz`.

When working with dates and times, programmers also need to consider leap years and leap seconds. There is a leap year every four years unless the year is divisible by 100 but not 400. This change keeps the calendar year in sync with the Earth's orbit around the sun. Inaccurate date calculations can result from failing to account for leap years, especially when working with historical data or long-term schedules. Occasionally added to UTC to compensate for Earth's rotation speed variations, Leap seconds present another challenge. While leap seconds are relatively rare, they can cause issues in high-precision timekeeping systems such as GPS networks and financial trading platforms.

Formatting and parsing dates are essential tasks in software development, especially when working with user interfaces, reports, and data exchange formats. Different cultures and countries use various date formats, leading to confusion if not handled properly. For example, in the United States, the common date format is MM/DD/YYYY, while in many other parts of the world, it is DD/MM/YYYY. Some systems use the ISO 8601 standard (YYYY-MM-DD) to avoid ambiguity and ensure consistency in data representation. Most programming languages provide functions to format dates according to different conventions. In Python, the `strftime` method allows developers to format date objects as strings, while the `strptime` function parses strings into date objects. Similarly, Java's `DateTimeFormatter` class enables flexible date formatting and parsing.

Date arithmetic is another critical aspect of handling dates and times. Many applications require calculations such as determining the number of days between two dates, adding or subtracting time intervals, or finding the day of the week for a given date. Most programming languages provide built-in functions to perform these operations efficiently. For example, in Python, the `time delta` class allows developers to add or subtract days, hours, or minutes from a given date. In Java, the `ChronoUnit` class provides methods to calculate differences between dates and times. Handling date arithmetic correctly is important in event scheduling, project management, and financial forecasting applications.

Databases play a crucial role in storing and managing date and time information. Most relational databases, such as MySQL, PostgreSQL, and SQL Server, include specialized data types for handling dates and times. These databases provide functions for comparing dates, extracting components such as year or month, and performing date arithmetic. One of the best database design practices is storing timestamps in UTC to ensure consistency and avoid issues related to time zone conversions. When querying date-related data, developers often need to consider indexing strategies to optimize performance, particularly when dealing with large datasets.

Synchronizing date and time information across distributed systems is a significant challenge in modern computing. In cloud-based applications and microservices architectures, multiple servers in different time zones must coordinate their operations while maintaining accurate time synchronization. Network Time Protocol (NTP) is commonly used to synchronize system clocks across different machines. Ensuring that all distributed system components operate on a consistent timeline is crucial for preventing errors in logging, transaction processing, and data consistency.

Real-world applications of handling dates and times extend to various domains, including finance, healthcare, transportation, and e-commerce. Accurate timestamps are essential for recording trades, tracking market fluctuations, and ensuring regulatory compliance in financial markets. In healthcare, electronic medical records rely on precise date and time information to document patient history, schedule appointments, and administer treatments. Transportation systems use time calculations for flight schedules, train departures, and GPS tracking. E-commerce platforms need accurate date and time handling for order processing, delivery estimates, and promotional events.

Challenges in handling dates and times can arise due to discrepancies between different calendar systems. While the Gregorian calendar is the most widely used system today, some applications must support alternative calendars such as the Islamic, Hebrew, or Chinese calendars. These calendars have different rules for determining months, leap years, and holidays, making date calculations more complex. Some programming languages and frameworks include support for multiple calendar systems to accommodate diverse user requirements.

Testing and debugging date and time-related code require careful attention to edge cases and potential pitfalls. Common issues include off-by-one errors when calculating date differences, incorrect handling of leap years, and failing to account for time zone differences. Automated testing frameworks often include features for simulating different time zones, adjusting system clocks, and verifying time-dependent logic. Writing unit tests that cover a wide range of scenarios helps ensure that date and time functionality behaves correctly under different conditions.

Best practices for handling dates and times in software development include using standardized formats, avoiding hardcoded time zone conversions, leveraging libraries for date manipulation, and documenting assumptions about time representation. Developers should also consider performance when working with large volumes of time-based data. Optimizing database queries, caching computed date values, and reducing unnecessary conversions can improve efficiency in time-sensitive applications.

Understanding how to handle dates and times effectively is crucial for building reliable, scalable, and user-friendly software systems. The complexities of time zones, daylight saving time, leap years, and different date formats require careful consideration to avoid errors and inconsistencies. By leveraging the tools and best practices available in modern programming languages and frameworks, developers can ensure that their applications accurately handle date and time information across various domains and use cases.

Error Handling and Debugging

For applications to be stable, dependable, and maintainable, error handling and debugging are crucial components of software development. No matter how skillfully a program is built, mistakes will inevitably occur, and knowing how to deal with them is essential. Incorrect user input, hardware malfunctions, network problems, and logical errors in code are just a few of the many possible causes of errors. To make sure the software works as intended, debugging is the process of finding, analyzing, and fixing these flaws. An essential part of the software development lifecycle, error handling, and debugging work together to help developers build reliable and resilient programs.

Syntax mistakes, runtime errors, and logical errors are the three main categories into which programming errors fall. When the code deviates from the computer language's grammatical rules, syntax problems arise. Usually, the compiler or interpreter finds these mistakes before the program is launched, stopping it from running until they are fixed. Some syntax errors include missing semicolons, misplaced parentheses, and improper variable definitions. Modern Integrated Development Environments (IDEs) offer real-time syntax checking and correction suggestions to assist developers in writing accurate code because these problems are generally simple to spot.

Runtime errors, sometimes referred to as exceptions, can result in an unexpected program termination while it is running. These errors occur when you try to open a file that doesn't exist, divide by zero, or access memory addresses that aren't there. In contrast to syntax errors, runtime errors only appear when the program is executed and are not discovered during compilation. Exception handling is one example of an effective error-handling technique that can keep these mistakes from crashing the program and give users insightful feedback. Most programming languages come with built-in exception-handling structures, such as try-catch blocks in Python and Java, to handle runtime mistakes gracefully and ensure the program keeps running even when anything goes wrong.

Since logical mistakes result in inaccurate output or unexpected behavior rather than software crashes, they are the hardest to identify. These mistakes are caused by logical problems in the software, such as erroneous computations, inappropriate loop usage, or defective decision-making frameworks. Because they might not be immediately noticeable and debugging them necessitates a thorough comprehension of the code and its expected behavior, logical mistakes can be especially troublesome. Developers frequently employ code reviews, unit tests, and debugging tools to find and fix logical flaws.

Developing user-friendly apps that offer concise, useful feedback when problems occur requires efficient error handling. By avoiding unexpected crashes and assisting users in fixing the problem, a well-thought-out error management strategy enhances the user experience. A well-handled error, for example, will show a meaningful message outlining the problem and recommending a solution when a user enters wrong data into a form. By verifying and cleaning user input, appropriate error handling in online applications helps stop security flaws like SQL injection and cross-site scripting attacks.

In contemporary programming languages, exception handling is a commonly used method for handling runtime failures. Developers can guarantee error management by enclosing potentially troublesome code in a try block and designating matching catch sections to handle particular exceptions. An exception-handling block in Python, for instance, would resemble this:

With the exception of ZeroDivisionError: print, try: result = 10 / 0.("Error: Division by zero is not allowed.")

This method clearly indicates the type of mistake and keeps the program from crashing. Exception handling can be used in more complicated applications to record mistakes, try unsuccessful operations again, or report serious malfunctions to higher system levels.

Another crucial component of error management and debugging is logging. Logging aids developers in identifying problems and determining their underlying causes by capturing error messages, stack traces, and other pertinent data. Log frameworks like Python's logging module, Node.js's Winston, and Java's Log4j offer strong real-time tools for recording and evaluating mistakes. To help prioritize issues and expedite debugging efforts, effective logging systems include classifying logs according to severity levels, such as debug, info, warning, error, and critical.

The methodical process of finding and fixing bugs in software is called debugging. Code inspection, debugging tools, and rigorous testing methods are some of the methods it entails. The use of print statements to monitor program execution and output variable values is one of the most popular debugging strategies. Despite its simplicity, this technique can be very useful for tracking a program's execution and spotting unusual behavior or wrong numbers.

Developers can establish breakpoints, walk through code execution, examine variable values, and examine call stacks using advanced debugging tools in modern development environments. IDEs like Visual Studio Code, PyCharm, and Eclipse have built-in debuggers that let developers halt execution at particular moments and thoroughly inspect the program state. Developers can identify the precise location of a mistake and comprehend how data moves through the application by iterating through the code line by line.

Another crucial debugging strategy that aids in the early detection of faults in the development process is unit testing. Developers may ensure their code operates as intended under various circumstances by creating automated tests for each program component. With testing frameworks like Mocha for JavaScript, pytest for Python, and JUnit for Java, developers can create test cases, run them automatically, and get real-time feedback on test results. By identifying faults before they are released into production, continuous integration techniques, which have tests run automatically anytime code changes are made, further improve software reliability.

Other methods that enhance error detection and debugging include code reviews and pair programming. Teams can find possible problems, exchange best practices, and improve overall code quality by having several developers review each other's work. Pair programming encourages real-time problem-solving and lowers the possibility of making mistakes by having two developers collaborate on the same code. These cooperative methods not only increase the effectiveness of debugging but also foster information exchange and skill improvement among team members.

Performance optimization also heavily relies on error handling and debugging. Memory leaks, performance snags, and excessive resource usage can all result from inefficient code. Profiling tools assist developers in evaluating their apps' functionality and pinpointing areas needing improvement. Developers can measure execution time, find memory leaks, and optimize code for greater performance with tools like Python's cProfile module, Valgrind for memory analysis in C and C++, and Chrome DevTools for web apps.

Another crucial component of error handling is security since badly handled errors can reveal weaknesses that hackers could take advantage of. Malicious users can exploit detailed error messages that expose system information, including file locations or database queries, to breach a system. To reduce security threats, developers should employ appropriate error-handling procedures, such as providing users with generic error messages and securely logging comprehensive error information. To further guard against unwanted access and guarantee data integrity, access controls, encryption, and input validation should be implemented.

Robust error handling and debugging techniques are becoming more and more crucial as software systems get more complicated. Error management in cloud-based applications and distributed systems needs to consider concurrency problems, network failures, and service outages. Applications are kept robust despite unforeseen shortcomings using techniques like circuit breakers, failover systems, and retries. Prometheus, Grafana, and AWS CloudWatch are observability solutions offering real-time monitoring and alerting, empowering developers to identify and address problems proactively.

Additionally, artificial intelligence and machine learning are enhancing error identification and debugging. Automated error detection systems use machine learning algorithms to examine logs, spot trends, and anticipate possible errors before they happen. Based on past data and industry best practices, AI-powered debugging aids like GitHub Copilot and DeepCode identify potential issues and offer real-time code recommendations.

To sum up, debugging and error handling are essential steps in software development that guarantee systems' dependability, security, and functionality. Developers can build durable and effective software systems by comprehending various error types, putting strong error-handling procedures in place, and using debugging tools and techniques. New developments in error management and debugging techniques will improve the capacity to identify, diagnose, and fix problems as technology develops, eventually producing more reliable and user-friendly programs.

CHAPTER III

The Document Object Model (DOM)

Introduction to the DOM

The Document Object Model, or DOM, is a fundamental idea in web development and programming. It facilitates the dynamic interaction between web content and programming languages like JavaScript by acting as a programming interface for web documents. An understanding of the DOM is essential for developers looking to construct responsive and dynamic web apps.

This section aims to give a thorough overview of the DOM by examining its composition, capabilities, and importance in contemporary web development. Fundamentally, a document's hierarchical structure—usually an HTML or XML document—is represented by the DOM. Since each node represents a section of the content, this structure is frequently compared to a tree. Thanks to the DOM's tree-like representation, developers can programmatically access and modify various web page elements. Nodes in this context can be text, attributes, components, or even comments, and each one contributes differently to the structure of the content. The document object is the entry point for working with the complete document and is the root of the DOM tree. The DOM's capacity to offer a language-neutral, platform-independent interface for viewing and modifying web documents is one of its main benefits. This makes the DOM a flexible tool for web development since developers may interact with it using a range of computer languages. However, because of its smooth interaction with web browsers, JavaScript is the most widely used language for DOM manipulation. Understanding how the DOM allows for dynamic content updates on web pages is essential to appreciating its importance. Web pages were static in the early days of the internet, which means that once they were loaded into a browser, their content remained unchanged. However, the DOM completely changed this paradigm by enabling developers to alter a web page's structure and content in real time. This dynamic flexibility is the foundation of contemporary online applications, incorporating features like animated user interfaces, real-time data changes, and interactive forms.

The ability to navigate the document tree is one of the fundamental ideas of the DOM. One must traverse the DOM's nodes to access certain elements or carry out operations on them. The DOM API has several attributes and methods that can be used to do this. The querySelector method enables more intricate selections using CSS-style selectors, whereas the getElementById function, for instance, enables developers to access an element by its unique identity. Developers can use these traversal techniques to identify particular document elements and perform focused changes. Developers can work with the DOM's structure and content and navigate it.

Adding, deleting, or changing text nodes, attributes, and other elements inside the document are all part of this manipulation. Developers can, for example, use the createElement method to create new elements, the setAttribute method to set their attributes, and the appendChild function to append them to the page. These procedures provide the foundation for developing dynamic and interactive web pages that react to user input and outside data sources. The DOM is also essential in managing events—actions or occurrences in the browser, including user interactions or resource loading. A key component of web development is event management, which allows programmers to react to user input and produce interactive experiences.

Using the DOM's powerful event model, developers may add event listeners to elements and define actions to do in response to particular events. To guarantee that a specific function is carried out when the button is clicked, a developer can, for instance, add a click event listener to the button element. Making web apps that are responsive and easy to use requires the use of this event-driven programming paradigm. The DOM has changed along with web development. The World Wide Web Consortium, or W3C, has established standards that modern web browsers use to implement the DOM. Thanks to these standards, developers may create code that functions flawlessly on several platforms guarantee consistency and interoperability between browsers. Furthermore, new features and APIs like the Shadow DOM and Custom Elements have been introduced due to DOM developments, allowing developers to design reusable and encapsulated web components. Even with all of its benefits, using the DOM is difficult. When working with huge and complex documents, one of the main concerns is the possibility of performance bottlenecks.

Modifying the DOM can be computationally costly, particularly when doing heavy operations or frequent updates. Developers frequently use debouncing, throttling, and virtual DOM implementations to lessen these performance problems. By reducing the effect of DOM modifications on overall application performance, these strategies help guarantee a responsive and seamless user experience. Cross-browser compatibility is an additional DOM difficulty. Even if contemporary browsers try to follow DOM standards, there may still be differences in how various browsers understand and use particular features. This may result in disparities in how web pages behave and look in various browsers. Developers frequently use feature detection and polyfills to overcome this difficulty and guarantee consistent behavior in various settings. While polyfills offer fallback implementations for features that might be absent in some browsers, feature detection entails determining whether the browser supports a particular feature before utilizing it. The DOM is utilized in many other situations, including server-side rendering and mobile app development, and is not just restricted to conventional web browsers. Using frameworks like Node.js, server-side rendering creates HTML content on the server and sends it to the client. In this case, the document structure is altered on the server using the DOM before being sent to the client. Similarly, mobile app development frameworks like React Native use web technology to create native mobile applications by utilizing DOM-like structures. This illustrates the DOM's adaptability and widespread use in contemporary program development. In recent years, the popularity of single-page apps, or SPAs, has highlighted the DOM's significance in web development. Web applications known as SPAs load a single HTML page and update its content dynamically while the user interacts with it. Full page reloads are no longer necessary using this method, which makes user experiences quicker and more fluid. A key component of SPAs is the DOM, which allows programmers to control the application's state and content dynamically. Frameworks such as Vue.js, Angular, and React offer tools and abstractions for effectively controlling the DOM in SPAs, streamlining development, and enhancing performance. The DOM will continue to change as the web does. Web Components and the HTML Template element are examples of emerging technologies and standards that promise to expand the DOM's functionality and make ever more complex web applications possible. For example, Web Components encourage modularity and code reuse by enabling developers to construct encapsulated and reusable custom elements with their own DOM and styling. On the other side, the HTML Template element makes it easier to create dynamic content by offering a means to specify and reuse sections of HTML syntax.

The continuous improvements in web development and the constantly shifting technological landscape are directly related to the DOM's future. The Document Object Model is a fundamental idea in web development that lets programmers make dynamic, interactive websites. It is an essential tool for contemporary web development because of its event-driven capabilities, flexible API, and hierarchical structure. Although there are some difficulties when working with the DOM, like cross-browser compatibility and performance snags, developers can use various strategies and best practices to overcome these issues. The DOM will continue to be essential to creating feature-rich, responsive, and user-friendly web applications as web technologies advance.

Manipulating the DOM

One of the most crucial abilities in web development is working with the Document Object Model or DOM. Each element of an HTML or XML document is treated as a node in the DOM, a structured document representation. Because of this representation, JavaScript may dynamically interact with a webpage's structure and content, allowing programmers to create responsive and highly interactive web apps. The foundation of front-end programming is the ability to work with the DOM, enabling dynamic content creation, real-time changes, and user interactions.

The browser builds the DOM tree, which shows the structure of the page's elements, after parsing the HTML when a webpage loads. Any HTML document element, attribute, and text passage within this tree becomes a node that JavaScript may access and change. Developers can add, remove, or modify components and properties dynamically without requiring a page reload, thanks to their ability to control the DOM. Form validation, single-page apps, and other interactive web experiences all depend on this.

Selecting items is a basic method of working with the DOM. JavaScript offers multiple ways to access particular document elements. One of the most often used functions is `getElementById()`, which enables developers to obtain an element by its unique ID. Calling `document.getElementById("header")`, for instance, yields the element with the ID "header," which can then be altered or worked with. `getElementsByClassName()` is another often used method that yields a group of elements that have the same class name. When several elements need to be focused at once, this is helpful. In the same way, `getElementsByTagName()` returns aspects according to their tag names, including all `

` or `

` elements in a document.

More robust and adaptable techniques for element selection were offered by modern JavaScript, specifically `querySelector()` and `querySelectorAll()`. Developers can choose the first matched element based on a CSS selector using the `querySelector()` method. This makes it extremely flexible since elements can be selected using class names, IDs, or tag names. `document.querySelector(".content")`, for instance, chooses the first element with the class "content." In contrast, the `querySelectorAll()` method returns a NodeList containing all matched nodes, which may be iterated to apply changes to each selected element.

Developers can alter an element's characteristics, content, or style after it has been chosen. The HTML content of an element can be directly modified using the `innerHTML` attribute. Setting `document.getElementById("message") is one example.outerHTML = "Hello, World!"` modifies the element's internal content using the ID "message." Similarly, to avoid accidentally injecting HTML code, the `textContent` attribute changes the text inside an element without interpreting it as HTML. The `setAttribute()` and `getAttribute()` methods also make changing an element's attributes simple. By modifying properties like `src`, `href`, `alt`, and `title`, developers may dynamically update tooltips, links, and pictures in response to user activities.

A web page's appearance can be changed quickly by modifying CSS styles through DOM manipulation. An element's inline styles can be accessed via the `style` property, allowing for the modification of characteristics, including color, background, font size, and visibility. An element with the ID "box" can have its background color changed to blue by using the code `document.getElementById("box").style.backgroundColor = "blue";`. However, directly altering inline styles isn't usually the most effective method, particularly when working with several items. Alternatively, dynamically adding or removing CSS classes may be more efficient. With the help of methods like `add()`, `remove()`, and `toggle()` provided by the `classList` property, developers can change class properties without affecting other styles. Calling `document.getElementById("button").classList.add("active")`, for example, applies predefined CSS rules associated with the "active" class to the specified element.

Dynamically adding and deleting elements is yet another potent DOM manipulation feature. Developers can construct new elements using the `createElement()` method, which can subsequently be added to the document using `appendChild()` or `insertBefore()`. This is very helpful for producing UI elements based on user input, adding additional form fields, and constructing dynamic lists. For instance, the following code can be used to create a new paragraph element and append it to a container:

`let newParagraph = document.createElement("p");` `newParagraph.textContent = "This is a dynamically added paragraph.";` `document.getElementById("container"). (newParagraph);` appendChild

Likewise, the `removeChild()` method and the `remove()` function can remove elements from the DOM. These techniques enable the deletion of components in response to user actions, like pressing the delete button in a to-do list app.

By reacting to user actions like clicks, mouse movements, keystrokes, and form submissions, events are essential to DOM manipulation and enable developers to create interactive web pages. Attaching event handlers to elements is made flexible using the `addEventListener()` method, which guarantees that particular methods run in response to an event. For instance, here's how to add a click event to a button:

"myButton" in `document.getElementById."click", addEventListener(function() {` {alert("Button clicked!");` {});`

Another key idea in event management is event delegation. Developers can use event bubbling to manage interactions between child elements and attach an event listener to a parent element rather than separately adding event listeners to each component. Performance is enhanced, and superfluous event bindings are decreased, particularly when working with dynamically created elements.

To update the webpage with fresh information, asynchronous operations—like retrieving data from an API —frequently call for DOM manipulation. JavaScript offers the Fetch API and XMLHttpRequest to update the DOM dynamically and get data from external sources. For instance, a webpage can show real-time weather updates, stock market information, or user-generated material without requiring a complete reload by utilizing `fetch()`.

`fetch("https://api.example.com/data")` `.then(response => response.json())` `.then(data => {` ~document.getElementById("info").textContent = data.message;` }});`

By guaranteeing that content updates seamlessly without interfering with the page's current state, this asynchronous technique improves user experience.

Modern front-end frameworks like React, Angular, and Vue.js rely heavily on DOM manipulation. By employing a virtual DOM to optimize DOM interactions, these frameworks reduce the need for direct manipulation of the real DOM and enhance performance. The virtual DOM minimizes needless reflows and repaints by enabling changes to be computed in memory before being effectively updated in the real DOM. Frameworks offer a more organized method of managing state management and UI updates, even though basic JavaScript DOM manipulation is still quite effective.

When modifying the DOM, security is crucial, especially when working with user-generated content. Applications may be vulnerable to cross-site scripting (XSS) attacks, in which malicious scripts are injected into the webpage if HTML is directly inserted using `innerHTML`. Developers can reduce this risk by implementing Content Security Policies (CSP) to limit the execution of untrusted scripts, sanitizing input, and using `textContent` rather than `innerHTML` when working with user input.

Another crucial component of DOM manipulation is performance optimization since making too many changes might result in slow rendering and a bad user experience. Performance can greatly increase by limiting reflows and repaints, batching changes, and reducing pointless DOM updates. More effective and responsive apps can be achieved by applying CSS transitions rather than JavaScript animations, caching DOM references, and using document fragments.

In summary, DOM manipulation is a key component of web development, which makes it possible to create dynamic and engaging user experiences. Developers can construct extremely responsive applications that adjust to user interactions and real-time data using JavaScript to select, alter, and manage items. Building contemporary online apps requires knowing how to handle events, work with the DOM effectively, and maximize performance. Best practices for DOM manipulation are improving as technology advances, guaranteeing that web apps stay quick, safe, and easy to use.

Event Handling in JavaScript

A key component of JavaScript programming that lets programmers make responsive and dynamic websites is event management. It allows recording and controlling user interactions and other events, like keyboard strokes, mouse clicks, and browser window modifications. Developers may create a rich, captivating experience by reacting to these events and updating the user interface dynamically. Since event management is the cornerstone of creating contemporary web applications, any JavaScript developer must understand it.

In JavaScript, an event is a browser activity or occurrence brought on by user input or other circumstances. Every event has a corresponding event object containing details about the event, including its type, the target element, and any pertinent metadata. Capturing these events, processing the related event objects, and carrying out the necessary responses are all part of event handling. Three primary steps are usually involved in event handling: specifying the event handler code, connecting an event listener, and choosing the target element.

The HTML element with which the event will be connected is the target element. This could be an input field, button, link, or any other element on the website. A function that watches for a certain event on the target element and initiates the associated event handler function when the event takes place is known as an event listener. The code that will be run in reaction to the event, such as processing user input or altering the user interface, is contained in the event handler function. The addEventListener function is one of the most popular ways to connect event listeners in JavaScript. The target element, the kind of event to watch for, and the event handler function to run when the event happens can all be specified by developers using this method. Compared to the more traditional inline event handler properties like on click or mouseover, the addEventListener method offers a better separation of concerns. It enables the attachment of numerous event listeners to a single element.

Another key idea in event management that can enhance web application performance and maintainability is event delegation. Attaching a single event listener to a parent element and utilizing it to manage events for several child components is known as event delegation. This method uses the idea of event bubbling, which describes how events spread from the target element to its ancestors up the DOM tree. Event delegation can simplify dynamic content management and minimize the number of event listeners required by recording events at a higher level in the DOM. Because it enables developers to manage events for items that are dynamically added or withdrawn from the DOM without extra event listeners, event delegation is especially helpful for managing events on these elements.

A fundamental idea in event handling is event propagation, which deals with how events flow across the DOM tree. The catching and bubbling phases are the two stages of event propagation. During the capturing phase, the event moves from the DOM tree's root to the target element. The event moves from the target element to the DOM tree's root during the bubbling phase. Event listeners on parent elements can handle events initiated by child elements because most events propagate in the bubbling phase by default. With the help of techniques like stopPropagation and stopImmediatePropagation, developers may regulate how events spread. While the stopImmediatePropagation method stops the event from propagating and stops additional event listeners on the same element from being activated, the stopPropagation method stops the event from propagating any further. These techniques can assist in avoiding unintended side effects and conflicts while giving developers fine-grained control over event handling.

Working with several kinds of events, including form, keyboard, mouse, and custom events, is another aspect of event management in JavaScript. Clicking, double-clicking, and mouse movement are examples of mouse events. Actions like pressing or releasing a key are examples of keyboard events. Form elements, such as submitting a form or altering the value of an input field, are connected to form events. The dispatchEvent method and the CustomEvent constructor can manage and trigger user-defined or custom events. Because every kind of event has distinct traits and applications, developers must be able to manage them efficiently.

Buttons, sliders, and drag-and-drop capability are interactive user interfaces frequently made using mouse events. For instance, handling a button's click event enables programmers to run code in reaction to a user clicking the button, displaying a modal window, or submitting a form. More intricate interactions can also be made with mouse events, including dragging and dropping components within a web page. Developers may produce rich and captivating user experiences that improve the functioning of their web apps by recording and reacting to mouse events.

When a user types text into a field or uses the arrow keys to navigate, keyboard events record and react to that input. For instance, handling a key-down event enables programmers to run code in response to a key press by the user, validating form information or starting a search. Because they would allow developers to provide alternate input methods and guarantee that their programs are useable with a keyboard, keyboard events are crucial for developing accessible web applications that people with impairments can use. Developers can produce accessible and responsive web apps that serve a wide variety of users by recording and reacting to keyboard events.

Inputs, checkboxes, and select elements are examples of form elements that are connected to form events. These events are utilized to submit forms, verify user input, and alter the user interface in response to form data. For instance, when a user submits a form, developers can run code that validates the input data and sends it to a server by handling a submit event on the form. Form events are necessary to create interactive, user-friendly forms that offer validation and feedback. Developers can design forms that assist users with the input process and guarantee that the data they provide is valid and comprehensive by recording and reacting to form events.

The dispatchEvent method and the CustomEvent constructor can manage and trigger user-defined or custom events. A versatile method for establishing unique interactions and communication between various application components is through custom events. To indicate that a particular action has been finished, such as loading data from a server or finishing user registration, developers can, for instance, construct a custom event. Developers can produce modular, decoupled code that is simpler to maintain and expand by utilizing custom events. Custom events are especially helpful when developing intricate systems with numerous components that must communicate with one another.

JavaScript's event handling is essential for handling promises, asynchronous activities, and basic interactions. Programming asynchronously entails operations that require time to finish, including reading a file or retrieving data from a server. To keep the application responsive and effective, developers can use event handling to run code in reaction to these asynchronous processes being finished. For instance, developers can process the answer and modify the user interface by managing the load event while retrieving data from a server.

Another crucial component of JavaScript event handling is error management. When an error arises during script execution or resource loading, error events are set off. Developers can design fallback mechanisms, log errors for debugging, and give users feedback by handling error events. For web applications to be strong and durable and manage unforeseen problems gracefully, error handling is crucial. Developers can produce programs that improve user experience and continue to function even when problems occur by recording and reacting to error occurrences.

The ability to generate and handle custom events is another essential component of JavaScript event management. The dispatchEvent method and the CustomEvent constructor can be used to manage and trigger user-defined or custom events. A versatile method for establishing unique interactions and communication between various application components is through custom events. Developers can produce modular, decoupled code that is simpler to maintain and expand by utilizing custom events. Custom events are especially helpful when developing intricate systems with numerous components that must communicate with one another.

Understanding and controlling the event loop, a fundamental idea in JavaScript's execution mechanism, is another aspect of event management. The event loop is in charge of handling events, controlling code execution, and carrying out asynchronous tasks. Developers can create more responsive and effective programs by comprehending how the event loop operates. The event loop continuously checks the call stack and event queue. The event loop pulls the subsequent event from the event queue and pushes its corresponding callback function onto the call stack for execution when it is empty. This procedure guarantees that the application stays responsive and that asynchronous activities are carried out in the proper order.

Event handling is a key component of developing dynamic and interactive web applications with JavaScript. Developers can create programs that offer a rich and captivating user experience by recording and reacting to user interactions and other events. Event management enables programmers to handle mistakes, manage asynchronous processes, design responsive user interfaces, and build unique interactions between various application components. Since event management is the cornerstone of creating contemporary web applications, any JavaScript developer must understand it.

Event handling is a crucial component of JavaScript programming that lets programmers make responsive and dynamic websites. Event handling enables programmers to create programs that can respond to user input, carry out activities, and update the user interface in real time by recording and reacting to user interactions and other events. Developing rich and captivating user experiences requires understanding the fundamental ideas of event handling, including event propagation, event delegation, and custom events. Additionally, event handling is essential for resolving mistakes, controlling asynchronous processes, and writing modular, decoupled programs. Any JavaScript developer must become proficient in event handling, which is the cornerstone of creating cutting-edge online apps that offer a smooth and pleasurable user experience. Developers may produce useful web apps that provide a rich and captivating user experience, enhancing their appeal and usability by utilizing event management effectively.

Working with Forms and User Input

A fundamental component of web development is working with forms and user input, enabling programmers to build dynamic, interactive apps to gather and process user data. Many web applications rely on forms to allow users to submit requests, make choices, and supply information. Developers may produce responsive and user-friendly web applications that satisfy the expectations of their customers by knowing how to work with forms and process user input efficiently.

Forms are HTML components that let users enter data using a variety of input fields, including text boxes, radio buttons, checkboxes, and dropdowns. The element that encloses these input fields establishes the parameters of the form and offers a way to send the data to a server for processing. The element's action and method specify the URL to which the form data should be submitted and the HTTP method (GET or POST) used to submit the form data, respectively, are contained in the element. Developers can design interfaces that make data collecting and user interaction easier by specifying the behavior and structure of forms.

Choosing the right input fields for the gathered data and arranging them logically and intuitively is essential to creating user-friendly forms. For instance, developers might utilize text boxes for names, radio buttons for gender, checkboxes for interests, and dropdowns for choosing a nation for gathering personal data. Developers may produce forms that are simple to use and fill out by carefully selecting and organizing the input fields, which will improve the user experience overall.

Working with forms requires validating user input to ensure the information users supply is correct and comprehensive. JavaScript can be used for client-side validation, while server-side scripting languages like PHP or Python can be used for server-side validation. Before submitting the form, client-side validation entails examining the input fields for particular requirements, such as necessary fields, valid email addresses, and numeric values. Users may fix any mistakes before the form is submitted, thanks to the instant feedback this gives them. Before processing the form input further, server-side validation entails verifying that it satisfies the requirements on the server after it has been submitted. Developers can guarantee the integrity and correctness of the data gathered via forms by carrying out client-side and server-side validation.

Handling form submission is one of the most important aspects of working with forms. The information submitted in the input fields of a form is transmitted to the server for processing when a user submits it. Depending on the type of data and the required level of security, either the GET or POST method can be used for this. While the POST method transmits the form data in the HTTP request body, keeping it hidden from the user, the GET method appends the form data to the URL, making it visible in the browser's address bar. Based on the particular needs of the application and the sensitivity of the data, developers must select the best technique for submitting the form.

The form data must be properly handled and stored after it is sent to the server. Depending on the application's needs, this could entail delivering the data by email, saving it to a database, or taking other steps. Server-side scripting languages like PHP, Python, or Node.js usually handle form data processing. These programming languages offer libraries and functions for sending emails, working with databases, and carrying out server-side tasks. Developers may guarantee that form data is safely managed and available for use in the future by processing and storing it on the server.

Managing many kinds of user input, including text, numbers, dates, and files, is another aspect of working with forms. Different input types call for distinct handling strategies to guarantee that the data is correctly recorded and processed. For instance, developers may need to sanitize information in text input fields where users might enter alphanumeric characters to guard against security flaws like SQL injection and cross-site scripting (XSS) attacks. Developers may need further computations or formatting based on the numeric data, and numeric input fields must be validated to guarantee that the provided values are legitimate numbers. Data input fields must be validated to ensure that the dates entered are within the permitted range and in the proper format. Users can upload files using file input fields; developers must manage file uploads securely to guard against fraudulent uploads and guarantee that the files are kept correctly.

More sophisticated methods, such as AJAX (Asynchronous JavaScript and XML), which enables asynchronous form submission without reloading the page, can also gather user input. With the help of AJAX, developers may produce responsive and dynamic web apps that offer a flawless user experience. Without requiring a complete page refresh, developers can use AJAX to send form data to the server and get a response. This speeds up the processing of form inputs and improves the user experience by giving instant feedback. When working with AJAX, developers can design interactive and effective forms using JavaScript to send HTTP requests to the server and handle the server's response.

Giving consumers feedback based on their input is crucial to working with forms. This can involve giving users real-time feedback while interacting with the form, displaying success messages for successful form submissions, and displaying error messages for invalid input. Developers may assist users in filling out forms and fixing any mistakes by giving them prompt, unambiguous feedback. This guarantees the accuracy and completeness of the data gathered via forms and improves the user experience overall.

Another important factor to consider when working with forms and user input is accessibility. Forms must be accessible to all users, including those with disabilities, according to developers. This entails enabling keyboard navigation and screen reader assistance, employing semantic HTML components, and giving input fields informative names. Developers may design inclusive forms that are useable by a wide variety of users by adhering to accessibility best practices. This guarantees adherence to accessibility guidelines and standards while enhancing the user experience.

Working with forms and user input raises serious security concerns as well. Developers must take precautions against harmful attacks and unauthorized access to the data gathered through forms. This entails employing secure server-side processing strategies, cleaning and verifying user input, and implementing secure form submission procedures. To guarantee the integrity and confidentiality of the data, common security flaws like SQL injection, cross-site scripting (XSS), and cross-site request forgery (CSRF) must be fixed. Developers may construct secure online applications and safeguard user data by adhering to security best practices.

Using contemporary web technologies like HTML5, CSS3, and JavaScript libraries to improve the user experience is another facet of dealing with forms. HTML5's introduction of additional input types and properties makes more flexibility over form behavior and validation possible. For instance, the pattern attribute can specify a regular expression for input validation, and the needed attribute can be used to make input fields mandatory. Form styling and visual feedback, including highlighting invalid input fields or showing personalized error messages, can be accomplished with CSS3. JavaScript libraries like jQuery and React offer additional features for making dynamic and interactive forms. By utilizing these technologies, developers may produce cutting-edge, intuitive forms that improve the user experience.

Another crucial component of working with forms and user input is testing. To ensure that forms work properly and respond to user input as intended, developers must carefully test them. This entails validating various input scenarios, including edge cases, valid and invalid data, and numerous input formats. Form behavior can be checked and user interactions can be simulated with automated testing tools like Cypress and Selenium. Before releasing the program, developers can find and address problems through thorough testing, guaranteeing that forms function dependably and offer a satisfying user experience.

Managing the state and keeping track of the user's progress is also part of handling user input and form data. Maintaining the status of the input fields and tracking the user's progress is crucial in complex forms with several phases or sections. This can be accomplished by employing strategies like storing intermediate data in hidden fields, saving the form data to local storage, or preserving the state in a client-side framework like Angular or React. Developers can produce a smooth and intuitive user experience by controlling the form's state and saving the user's progress.

Developers must consider the performance effects of working with forms and user input and managing the state. To provide a responsive user experience, form submissions, and user input must be handled efficiently. This entails reducing the number of network requests, processing form data as efficiently as possible, and ensuring the user interface stays responsive when interacting with the form. Form performance and user input handling can be enhanced with strategies including debouncing input events, delayed loading form components, and server-side processing optimization.

When working with forms and user input, localization and internationalization are crucial factors. Supporting different languages and regional formats is vital for web apps that aim to reach a worldwide audience. This entails managing regional variations in date, time, and number formats in addition to translating form labels, validation messages, and other text elements into various languages. Developers may make forms that are accessible and easy to use for users from multiple geographical locations and cultural backgrounds by putting internationalization and localization into practice.

Managing edge circumstances and unforeseen situations is another aspect of working with forms and user input. Users may move away from the form before finishing it, provide unexpected or inaccurate data, or have network issues when submitting the form. Developers must foresee and manage these situations to guarantee a solid and dependable user experience. This may entail putting in place fallback procedures, displaying unambiguous error warnings, and enabling users to store their work for later use. Developers can design robust forms that offer a satisfying user experience by managing edge situations and unforeseen circumstances.

In summary, a key component of web development that helps programmers create dynamic and interactive web applications is dealing with forms and user input. The main tool for gathering user input is a form that enables users to interact with online apps, submit requests, and supply information. Creating responsive and captivating user experiences requires creating user-friendly forms, validating and processing user input, handling form submissions, and delivering feedback. To improve the functionality and usability of forms, developers must also take accessibility, security, and contemporary online technologies into account. Developers can produce web apps that efficiently gather and handle data by being proficient in these areas.

CHAPTER IV

Asynchronous JavaScript

Understanding Asynchronous Programming

Asynchronous programming is a key idea in contemporary software development that allows programs to run several tasks simultaneously without interfering with the main thread of execution. Enhancing the effectiveness, responsiveness, and scalability of applications—especially those that depend on networking, real-time processing, or user interactions—requires this strategy. A thorough examination of asynchronous programming's tenets, execution models, benefits, and implementation difficulties is necessary.

Programming has historically been done using a synchronous model, in which each operation is carried out one after the other. According to this paradigm, the program stops running when a function is called until it has finished its duty. Despite being straightforward, this method frequently results in inefficiencies, particularly when handling waiting-intensive operations like file I/O, database queries, or network requests. To solve these inefficiencies, asynchronous programming was created, which greatly enhances performance and resource usage by enabling activities to run independently and concurrently.

Non-blocking execution is a fundamental idea in asynchronous programming. Asynchronous programming permits the execution of other activities while awaiting the completion of lengthy processes, in contrast, synchronous programming requires tasks to finish before moving on to the next instruction. This is especially helpful in web development, as applications often need to process several user inputs simultaneously, constantly change user interfaces, and retrieve data from distant locations. By utilizing asynchronous programming, developers may ensure that apps stay responsive and effective even when faced with demanding workloads.

Callbacks, promises, and async/await are just a few of the paradigms and methods used in asynchronous programming. One of the first techniques to provide asynchronous behavior was callbacks. When a function is supplied as an argument to another function, it is called back once the original function has finished its task. Despite their effectiveness, callbacks frequently result in "callback hell," where several nested callbacks produce challenging code to comprehend, maintain, and debug.

The idea of promises was presented to lessen the difficulties brought on by callbacks. A value that might be accessible now, later, or never at all is represented by a promise. It enables developers to attach handlers that run when the promise is fulfilled or refused, making handling asynchronous tasks clearer and easier. This method makes it easier to manage several asynchronous processes in an organized way by improving code readability and lowering complexity.

The async/await syntax, which further streamlines asynchronous code, was developed due to the growth of asynchronous programming. Developers can create asynchronous code that looks like synchronous code by using async/await, which makes it simpler to understand and more intuitive. The await keyword allows developers to handle asynchronous tasks more linearly and legibly by pausing execution until the promise is resolved. An async function always returns a promise. This paradigm change has greatly improved how developers design and maintain asynchronous code in contemporary programming languages like JavaScript, Python, and C#.

Despite its benefits, developers face several difficulties while using asynchronous programming. Managing race conditions, which arise when several asynchronous jobs try to alter shared resources simultaneously, is one of the main difficulties. Unpredictable behavior, corrupted data, and difficult-to-debug faults can result from race circumstances. Developers frequently employ synchronization techniques like locks, semaphores, and atomic operations to synchronize access to shared resources and avoid unforeseen conflicts to solve this problem.

Error management presents another difficulty in asynchronous programming. Using structures like try/catch blocks, handling errors in synchronous programming is simple. Asynchronous programming is more difficult to handle since errors can arise at various stages of the execution flow. The catch method in promises offers built-in error-handling capabilities, and async/await enables try/catch blocks in asynchronous methods. Proper error handling is crucial for applications to stay resilient and recover gracefully from unplanned failures.

Because of its non-linear execution pattern, debugging asynchronous code is more challenging than debugging synchronous code. Because breakpoints and stack traces can get complicated when working with asynchronous activities, traditional debugging tools and techniques might be useless. Modern development environments provide specific debugging tools and logging methods to help developers overcome these obstacles and efficiently detect problems by tracking down asynchronous execution.

Another important component of asynchronous programming is performance optimization. Performance bottlenecks may result from incorrect implementation of asynchronous execution, even though it increases efficiency by permitting concurrent task execution. To guarantee optimum performance, developers must carefully control resource allocation, avoid unnecessary context switching, and reduce memory overhead. Strategies like batching, throttling, and debouncing are frequently employed to maximize asynchronous workflows and avoid needless performance loss.

Microservices architectures and distributed systems both heavily rely on asynchronous programming. Since services in these settings frequently interact with one another over networks, asynchronous communication is crucial to preserving scalability and responsiveness. Asynchronous APIs, event-driven structures, and message queues are commonly used to let distributed components communicate with one another. This keeps services separate and allows them to manage high concurrency levels effectively.

The emergence of serverless computing has further highlighted the significance of asynchronous programming. Serverless solutions that scale automatically according to workload, like AWS Lambda and Azure Functions, perform tasks as needed. These platforms are ideal for event-driven applications, real-time data processing, and background job execution because they mainly rely on asynchronous execution to manage several concurrent requests without using resources.

Asynchronous programming is also very beneficial for front-end web development. Real-time updates, dynamic content loading, and fluid animations are all common requirements for modern web applications. Thanks to asynchronous programming, developers can manage user interactions, retrieve data from APIs, and change the user interface (UI) without generating delays or freezing the application. Asynchronous programming patterns are widely used by frameworks such as React, Angular, and

Vue.js to improve performance and preserve a responsive user experience.

Asynchronous programming is essential for handling background processes, controlling network requests, and enhancing battery life in mobile app development. Mobile applications commonly interface with distant servers to retrieve data, transmit notifications, and synchronize user information. Asynchronous execution ensures that these processes don't interfere with the user interface, resulting in a seamless and continuous experience. Asynchronous APIs and background processing features are offered by platforms such as iOS and Android to make mobile app development more effective.

Asynchronous programming is frequently used in AI and machine learning applications to efficiently process data and train models. Processing big datasets, executing computationally demanding algorithms, and carrying out parallel calculations are common steps in training machine learning models. These operations can operate concurrently thanks to asynchronous programming, which minimizes processing time and maximizes resource use. Asynchronous execution is used by frameworks such as TensorFlow and PyTorch to improve performance in deep learning applications.

Asynchronous programming is useful in large data processing and cloud computing, where enormous volumes of data need to be handled concurrently. Asynchronous execution is essential for distributed computing frameworks like Apache Spark and Hadoop to manage massive data processing jobs effectively. These frameworks are perfect for data-intensive applications because they achieve high speed and scalability by dividing workloads among several nodes and carrying out activities asynchronously.

Implementing asynchronous programming also involves security considerations. Vulnerabilities like timing attacks, race situations, and resource exhaustion can be introduced by asynchronous execution. To reduce potential risks and guarantee that asynchronous applications stay safe and impervious to assaults, developers must implement the right security measures, such as input validation, access control, and rate restriction.

As programming languages, frameworks, and development tools advance, so does asynchronous programming. Reactive programming, which expands on asynchronous concepts, has become more popular recently. By emphasizing event-driven, non-blocking execution, reactive programming helps programmers create scalable and incredibly responsive programs. The possibilities of contemporary software development are further enhanced by libraries like RxJS, Project Reactor, and Akka Streams, which offer strong abstractions for managing asynchronous data streams.

Building effective, scalable, and responsive apps requires developers to have a solid understanding of asynchronous programming. Developers can design systems that efficiently manage concurrent tasks while preserving code readability and maintainability by utilizing non-blocking execution, promises, async/await, and reactive programming concepts. Race situations, error handling, and debugging complexity are some difficulties that asynchronous programming can bring. Still, these problems can be lessened with the right implementation techniques and industry best practices. Asynchronous programming will continue to be a fundamental component of software development as technology develops, allowing for the production of high-performance programs that satisfy the requirements of contemporary computer environments.

Working with Promises

In contemporary JavaScript development, working with promises is crucial, especially with asynchronous programming. An object that symbolizes an asynchronous activity's eventual success or failure is called a promise. Asynchronous programming enables time-consuming operations, like reading files or retrieving data from an API, to be carried out without interfering with the remainder of the code. This results in better responsiveness, enhanced performance, and a more seamless user experience. Writing clear, maintainable, and productive JavaScript applications requires understanding promises and the ability to interact with them effectively.

In JavaScript, a promise has a defined lifecycle. A promise is first formed in the pending state, which indicates that the task has not yet been finished. If the operation is successful, it can go into a fulfilled state; if an error occurs, it can go into a rejected state. A promise cannot change its state once it has been resolved, whether successfully or badly. This immutability is a potent tool for managing intricate activities since it guarantees predictability while handling asynchronous actions.

Working with promises is mostly accomplished by chaining the `.then()`, `.catch()`, and `.finally()` methods. A callback function that gets the resolved value is executed by the `.then()` method in order to manage a fulfilled promise. Developers can successively chain several asynchronous operations with this technique. For instance, a `.then()` block can process the response data from an API request. The `.catch()` method handles the promise's rejection in the event of an error. It takes the error as a parameter and lets developers do what needs to be done, including showing users error messages or performing the process again. The `.finally()` method is helpful for cleanup chores like hiding loading indications because it is run regardless of whether the promise was accepted or denied.

Promises have the important benefit of preventing the notorious "callback hell," which happens when several nested callbacks make the code hard to comprehend and maintain. Asynchronous tasks can be organized more legibly and linearly by using promises. Developers can chain `.then()` statements in place of highly nested callback methods, which makes the code easier to handle. Promise chaining, for instance, makes it easy to organize processes such as receiving user data from a server and then getting more information based on the initial response.

`Promise.all()` is another crucial promise feature that enables the execution of several promises simultaneously. Taking an array of promises, this method returns a new promise that either rejects if any of the input promises fail or resolves when all promises have been resolved. When several separate API requests must be made at once, this helps to increase efficiency by preventing needless sequential execution. Error handling is essential since the entire promise chain is rejected if any promises in `Promise.all()` are refused.

`Promise.allSettled()` offers a solution for situations where developers wish to continue with the remaining promises even if some fail. This method produces an array of objects that describe each promise's outcome, whether fulfilled or refused, in contrast to `Promise.all()`. This is especially helpful in situations where partial success is acceptable, such as loading several resources, where some may fail without impairing an application's overall functioning.

`Promise.race()` is another helpful technique that resolves or rejects as soon as the array's first promise settles. This is advantageous when putting timeout systems in place where the quickest reaction is required.

To ensure a faster user experience, `Promise.race()` can be used, for instance, to retrieve the response from the quickest source when numerous API endpoints give similar data.

Another variant, `Promise.any()`, ignores rejected promises and returns the first fulfilled promise out of the list. This is helpful when several sources provide data, and the objective is to recover the first successful response without being impacted by failures.

The `Promise` constructor, which accepts a function with two parameters, `resolve` and `reject`, creates a custom promise. While the `reject` function indicates an error and initiates the `.catch()` method, the `resolve` function fulfills the promise by providing the outcome to the `.then()` method. This gives developers more control over the execution flow by enabling them to encapsulate asynchronous activities within a promise.

Working with promises has been even easier with JavaScript's introduction of `async` and `await`, which make asynchronous code appear and act more like synchronous code. Developers can avoid using numerous `.then()` chains by declaring a function as `async`, which allows them to utilize the `await` keyword to suspend execution until a promise resolves. Code becomes simpler and easier to read, particularly when handling several asynchronous tasks. However, since exceptions thrown inside an `async` function will be interpreted as rejected promises, it is crucial to manage problems appropriately using `try` and `catch` blocks.

For programs to be reliable, error management in promises is essential. Application crashes may occur if a pledge is refused and the issue is not handled appropriately, leaving unhandled promise rejections. This can be avoided by enclosing `await` calls in `try-catch` blocks or using `.catch()`. Furthermore, application stability increases by recording faults and offering fallback options like retrying unsuccessful requests or showing pertinent error information.

Additionally, promises are essential to contemporary web development frameworks and libraries. For example, promises are frequently used in React to retrieve data from APIs, and Redux-Thunk and other state management tools depend on them to manage asynchronous operations. Promises are a common tool in Node.js for handling asynchronous file operations, database searches, and API calls. Working with asynchronous data is simpler because of the built-in support for promises offered by several libraries, like Axios.

Handling asynchronous operation sequences requires an understanding of promise chaining. Developers can easily transmit data from one operation to another because each `.then()` method yields a new promise. When retrieving data that depends on prior responses, this is especially helpful. For instance, promise chaining ensures that each step is finished before going on to the next while collecting a user's profile and then their recent activity.

`Array.prototype.reduce()` can be used in conjunction with promises to establish a controlled execution flow when developers need to carry out promises in a sequential manner instead of in parallel, eliminating needless API calls or activities. This method works well in situations where order is important since it guarantees that each promise will only be fulfilled after the one before it has been settled.

Another important factor to take into account while working with promises is performance optimization. Although promises are more efficient than typical callbacks, bottlenecks may be introduced by excessive chaining or poorly executed promises. Performance can be improved by carefully managing concurrent requests, minimizing pointless promise wrapping, and, when practical, using cache methods.

Better code modularity and reusability are also made possible by promises. Developers can design reusable components that manage particular activities, such as processing data, managing user authentication, or making API queries, by encapsulating asynchronous functionality into functions that yield promises. This modular strategy minimizes code duplication and improves maintainability.

Debugging promises can occasionally be difficult, particularly when working with lengthy promise chains. Tools like the "async stack trace" feature in developer consoles are available in modern browsers and aid in tracking the progression of asynchronous processes. Tracing promise execution and spotting problems can also be facilitated by adding logging statements inside the `.then()`, `.catch()`, and `finally()` sections.

Handling asynchronous processes while testing promises in unit tests properly is necessary. Several testing frameworks, including Jest and Mocha, support promises, which enable tests to wait for promises to resolve before issuing assertions. Using `async` and `await` in test situations guarantees that promises are handled correctly, avoiding race circumstances and inaccurate outcomes.

Promises have greatly enhanced JavaScript's handling of asynchronous programming by offering a methodical and reliable mechanism to control time-consuming processes. Working with promises has become much easier with the introduction of `async` and `await`, which have improved code readability and maintainability. Building effective and scalable applications requires understanding promise chaining, parallel execution techniques, error handling, and performance optimizations. Promises are still a fundamental component of contemporary web development as JavaScript develops further, guaranteeing that programs can manage asynchronous tasks efficiently while preserving a seamless user experience.

The Fetch API and AJAX

AJAX and the Fetch API are crucial tools for contemporary web development because they allow asynchronous data retrieval and web server interaction without necessitating a page reload. These technologies, which offer real-time data sharing, dynamic content changes, and a more seamless user experience, have completely changed how web applications operate. Developers creating responsive and effective web applications must thoroughly understand their functions, distinctions, and real-world uses.

In the early 2000s, AJAX—an acronym for Asynchronous JavaScript and XML—became a revolutionary technology. Web pages had to be completely reloaded to display updated data from a server before its introduction. This method produced a subpar user experience and was ineffective. By enabling JavaScript to send HTTP queries to a server, get data, and update only particular sections of a web page without necessitating a complete reload, AJAX revolutionized this. Faster, more interactive applications resulted from this, including web-based email clients that refresh inboxes without requiring page reloads, online forms that check input in real time, and live search suggestions.

The `XMLHttpRequest` (XHR) object, which enables asynchronous communication between JavaScript and a web server, is the foundation of traditional AJAX. Sending HTTP queries and receiving server responses—typically in the form of XML, JSON, or plain text—are made possible by the `XMLHttpRequest` object. Developers can handle the request synchronously or asynchronously; asynchronous requests are recommended because they don't block. Several event handlers are included in the XHR object, including `onreadystatechange`, which keeps track of modifications to the request state and takes the necessary action in response to the answer. Despite its strength, XHR can be difficult to use because of its verbose syntax and requirement for explicitly handling several states.

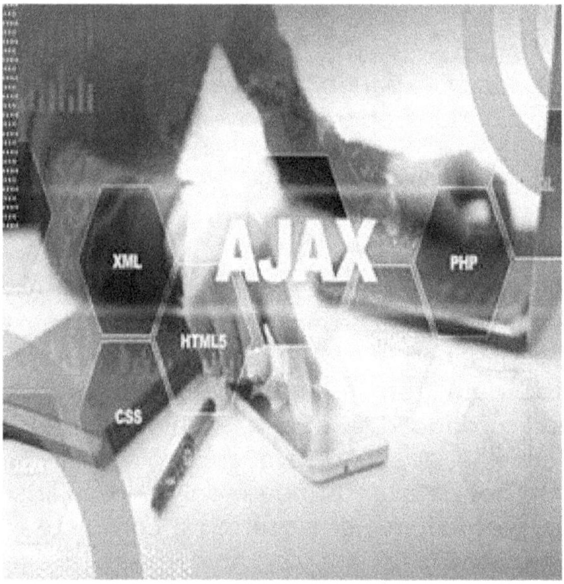

To simplify asynchronous data fetching and offer a more versatile and potent method of handling HTTP requests, the Fetch API was presented as a contemporary substitute for `XMLHttpRequest`. In contrast to XHR, the Fetch API is based on Promises, making asynchronous code easier to read and maintain. Using the `fetch()` method, which yields a Promise that resolves to the request's response, Fetch offers a simple syntax. With this method, developers may work with asynchronous data using simpler, easier-to-manage syntax and do away with the necessity for intricate event management.

The Fetch API's enhanced response processing is one of its main benefits. Fetch uses `Response` objects to represent responses, which provide methods for parsing data in different forms such as `text()`, `json()`, and `blob()`. Fetch enables developers to handle responses directly using the `.then()` method, which improves readability and reduces boilerplate code, in contrast to XHR, which necessitates checking several states and handling responses manually. For instance, Fetch is a more effective and developer-friendly option because it requires a few lines of code to retrieve data from an API endpoint and convert it to JSON.

Another important benefit is the Fetch API's support for contemporary features like streaming, custom headers, and enhanced error handling. Fetch simplifies error management by automatically rejecting a Promise in case of a network issue, unlike XHR, which does not reject requests depending on HTTP response statuses. Developers must manually verify the response status and handle issues appropriately because Fetch does not reject responses with HTTP error statuses like 404 or 500. This gives an application more control over how faults are handled.

AJAX and the Fetch API are frequently utilized in many web development contexts, especially when interacting with RESTful APIs. Web applications can use HTTP methods like GET, POST, PUT, and DELETE to communicate with servers through a REST API (Representational State Transfer). By sending HTTP queries, retrieving data, and dynamically changing web pages, Fetch facilitates communication with RESTful APIs. Applications that need to retrieve and display data without requiring a page reload, such social network feeds, online marketplaces, weather apps, and real-time notifications, frequently employ this feature.

AJAX and Fetch are frequently used for asynchronous form data submission. Form submission used to result in a complete page reload, which delayed the user experience. Developers can manage answers and transfer form data to a server without reloading the page using AJAX or Fetch. This enables seamless interactions, including showing success or error notifications or providing rapid validation messages without interfering with the user's workflow. By enabling form data to be supplied via the `FormData` object or JSON encoding, Fetch streamlines this procedure and simplifies handling various content types on the server side.

Another effective use of AJAX and Fetch is dynamically updating the DOM while retrieving data from an API. Many contemporary online apps rely on APIs to get real-time data, like market prices, sports scores, weather updates, and live chat conversations. Without requiring a complete page reload, developers may use Fetch to perform recurring API calls, process the response, and update particular page elements. Delivering real-time updates without interfering with other material improves the user experience.

The management of CORS (Cross-Origin Resource Sharing) is another crucial component of working with AJAX and Fetch. JavaScript cannot request a different domain unless the server specifically permits it due to security limitations in web browsers. CORS's security feature allows servers to define which domains can use cross-origin requests to access resources. The browser stops a Fetch request for security concerns if it is sent to a server without the appropriate CORS headers. The server's CORS settings can be changed by developers to permit cross-origin requests, guaranteeing that apps can safely communicate with external APIs.

When utilizing AJAX and the Fetch API, error management is essential. Server errors, incorrect API endpoints, network failures, and authentication problems can cause request failures. Instead of failing silently, applications that handle errors properly give users insightful feedback. While response statuses must be manually examined to handle issues like 404 Not Found or 500 Internal Server Error, errors may be managed with Fetch using `.catch()` to identify network failures. Web apps are more reliable when mistakes are logged and user-friendly notifications are displayed.

Even though Fetch has mostly supplanted XHR in contemporary development, legacy systems occasionally still use XMLHttpRequest because of compatibility issues. Because older browsers might not support Fetch entirely, developers may need to employ fallback solutions or polyfills to guarantee functioning. Additionally, XHR-based AJAX implementations are still used in certain older corporate systems and online applications, so developers must be knowledgeable about both technologies.

The `async` and `await` functions in JavaScript can be used to improve further asynchronous activities, such as Fetch and AJAX queries. `async` and `await`, which were first used in contemporary JavaScript, make working with Promises easier and enable asynchronous code to be written synchronously. To make code easier to read and debug, developers can use `await` to hold execution until a Promise resolves, rather than chaining numerous `.then()` methods. The use of `async` and `await` with Fetch helps to avoid deeply nested callback structures and enhances the clarity of asynchronous operations.

Another crucial factor to take into account while utilizing AJAX and Fetch is performance optimization. Performance bottlenecks may result from frequent API requests, particularly in applications with significant traffic. Caching, request throttling, and debouncing are among the strategies that assist in cutting down on pointless API requests and boosting productivity. While throttling restricts the frequency of API queries to avoid an excessive server load, local caching of responses can help prevent duplicate network requests. Debouncing ensures that API calls only happen after a predetermined time, which is very helpful for real-time filtering and search input fields.

Security is a major consideration when using AJAX and Fetch requests, especially when working with sensitive data. To avoid unwanted access, developers must ensure that API queries are correctly allowed and authenticated. Security concerns can be reduced by adopting token-based authentication, using HTTPS for secure connection, and verifying user input before transmitting requests. Safeguarding against common vulnerabilities like cross-site scripting (XSS) and cross-site request forgery (CSRF) when interacting with external APIs and managing user-generated content is crucial.

The way web applications communicate with servers has been greatly enhanced with AJAX's development and the Fetch API's release. Dynamic online content was made possible by AJAX. However data fetching has been updated with a more adaptable and effective method thanks to the Fetch API. Developers may create dependable and scalable web apps by knowing how to use these technologies efficiently, manage errors appropriately, maximize performance, and guarantee security best practices. Understanding Fetch and asynchronous JavaScript processes is crucial for developing quick, responsive, and engaging user experiences as the web grows.

Async/Await in JavaScript

JavaScript's strong and contemporary Async/Await functionality makes it easier for programmers to construct asynchronous code that is easier to read and maintain.

Because it allows developers to manage tasks that require waiting for external resources, such as network requests, file operations, or timers, without interfering with the main program's execution, asynchronous programming has become a crucial component of web development. Developers used promises and callbacks to handle asynchronous tasks before introducing Async/Await. Despite their effectiveness, these methods frequently produced complicated, hard-to-read code, sometimes called "callback hell" or "promise chains." With ECMAScript 2017 (ES8), Async/Await was added as a syntactic enhancement over promises, offering a more streamlined and user-friendly method of working with asynchronous code. The idea of asynchronous programming in JavaScript must be understood to appreciate the importance of Async/Await. JavaScript can only perform one task simultaneously because it is a single-threaded language. Every operation in a synchronous program is carried out one after the other, and the program must wait for one task to finish before proceeding to the next. Performance bottlenecks may result, particularly when handling laborious operations like retrieving data from a distant server. In contrast, asynchronous programming enables the software to carry out other tasks while it awaits the completion of an asynchronous operation. Callbacks and event loops are used to provide this non-blocking behavior. However, utilizing callbacks to manage asynchronous processes can easily get complicated, particularly when several nested callbacks are involved. ECMAScript 2015 (ES6) added promises to overcome the drawbacks of callbacks. An asynchronous operation's ultimate completion (or failure) is represented by a promise, which enables developers to attach handlers for the operation's success or failure. Promises give developers a more organized approach to working with asynchronous code, allowing them to use the then function to bind together several asynchronous tasks. Promises reduced some callback problems, but they still needed chaining, which could result in complicated and difficult-to-read code. Building on promises, Async/Await offers a more sophisticated and legible approach to working with asynchronous programming. An asynchronous function that implicitly returns a promise is declared with the async keyword. The await keyword in an async function can halt the function's execution until a promise is accepted or denied. This makes asynchronous code easier to read and comprehend by enabling developers to write it synchronously. One or more await expressions may be present in an async function; each awaited expression halts the function's execution until the associated promise is fulfilled. The ability of Async/Await to streamline error handling in asynchronous programs is one of its main advantages. To handle problems when utilizing promises, developers must include a catch handler in each promise chain. Async/Await, on the other hand, enables programmers to handle problems using try/catch blocks, much like in synchronous programming. This increases the code's general robustness and decreases the possibility of unhandled problems by making error handling simpler and more consistent. The distinction between handling asynchronous operations with promises and Async/Await is illustrated in the following example. Imagine a situation where we must retrieve information from a distant API and handle the result. With promises, the code could resemble this: .then(response => response.json()).then(data => { console.log(data); }) fetch('https://api.example.com/data') The code catch(error => { console.error('Error:', error); } Although this code works, it can become cumbersome for more complicated tasks because it chains several then and catches handlers together. The same thing may be accomplished more succinctly and readablely with Async/Await: async function fetchData() { try { const data = await response.json(); console.log(data); ` const response = await fetch('https://api.example.com/data');

capture (error) { console.error('Error:', error); } } The fetchData function is defined as an async function in this example, which enables the usage of await expressions to halt execution until the promises delivered by response.json() and fetch are fulfilled. A try/catch block to handle errors makes the code easier to comprehend and maintain.

When several asynchronous activities must be carried out either sequentially or concurrently, Async/Await excels. Imagine a scenario where we must retrieve information from two distinct APIs and merge the findings. With promises, the code could resemble this: Promise.all([fetch('https://api.example1.com/data'), fetch('https://api.example2.com/data')])).responses => Promise. all, then(response => response.json()))))).console.log(combinedData); }; then(data => { const combinedData = [...data[0],...data[1]]); }).catch(error => { console.error('Error:', error); }); Although this code achieves the intended functionality, it can be challenging to read and maintain because it nests promises inside a Promise.all call. The same task may be accomplished with Async/Await in a more user-friendly manner: fetchAndCombineData() async function { try { const [answer1, answer2] = await Const data1 = await response1.json(); const data2 = await response2.json(); const combined data = [...data1,...data2]; console.log(combined data); } Promise.all([fetch('https://api.example1.com/data'), fetch('https://api.example2.com/data')]); catch (error) { console.error('Error:', error); } } Retrieve and Combine Data; The fetchAndCombineData method in this example pauses execution until both fetch operations are finished using await expressions. After that, await is used to process the results sequentially, producing a code structure that is easier to read and maintain. Although Async/Await makes asynchronous programming easier, it should not be used in place of promises. Rather, it expands upon promises by offering a more intuitive vocabulary for interacting with them. The await keyword effectively "unwraps" the promise, enabling developers to work with the resolved value directly, even if async methods still return promises underneath. This indicates that comprehending Async/Await still requires a comprehension of promises. Another crucial characteristic is Async/Await's interoperability with current JavaScript capabilities and libraries. Async functions can be easily integrated with other promise-based APIs and tools because they return promises. As previously shown, developers can execute many asynchronous tasks simultaneously by combining Async/Await with the Promise.all method. Furthermore, well-known JavaScript libraries like Axios, which offers a promise-based interface for submitting HTTP requests, can be utilized with Async/Await. In conclusion, Async/Await is a strong and sophisticated JavaScript feature that simplifies asynchronous programming by offering a more understandable and manageable vocabulary. Async/Await simplifies the handling of promises and callbacks, enabling developers to create asynchronous code in a synchronous-like fashion. This makes managing asynchronous processes simpler.

Async/Await enables developers to build more reliable and intuitive online applications by handling sequential or concurrent operations, addressing errors, and integrating with pre-existing frameworks. A key component of contemporary web development is asynchronous programming, and any JavaScript developer would benefit from knowing Async/Await. Async/Await has grown to be a vital tool in the developer's toolbox because of its capacity to streamline code, increase readability, and improve error handling. Features like Async/Await will be essential in determining the direction of web development as JavaScript develops further, allowing programmers to create more effective, responsive, and manageable applications. Leveraging Async/Await's full potential and developing innovative web experiences requires understanding its advantages and workings. Recognizing that Async/Await is not a panacea is crucial, even if it has completely changed how developers manage asynchronous activities. In some situations, it might not be the best option to use Async/Await. For example, the overhead of utilizing Async/Await may result in performance problems when handling many small asynchronous jobs. In some situations, using lower-level strategies like callbacks or promises may be more effective. Developers should also be aware of potential performance-impacting problems such as inadvertent blocking or overuse of await within loops. Despite these factors, Async/Await is a useful technique for most asynchronous programming scenarios since its benefits greatly exceed its drawbacks. Like any programming feature, developers must know when and how to use Async/Await to maximize its advantages and minimize potential disadvantages. To sum up, Async/Await is a major improvement in how JavaScript developers manage asynchronous programming.

Async/Await makes working with promises and callbacks easier by offering a clearer and more intuitive syntax, making asynchronous code easier to manage and less prone to errors. It is an essential component of contemporary web development due to its ability to manage sequential and concurrent operations, enhance error handling, and interact with pre-existing libraries. The future of JavaScript and web development will surely be greatly influenced by Async/Await as developers continue to investigate and adopt it.

CHAPTER V

JavaScript in the Browser

Browser Storage and Cookies

To improve user experience, preserve application state, and boost website performance, browser storage, and cookies are essential elements of web development. Thanks to these techniques, developers can keep data on the client side, making surfing more effective and customized. Web developers must comprehend browser storage and cookies since they enable efficient user information management and data persistence between sessions. The many facets of browser storage and cookies are examined in this section, along with their applications, benefits, and difficulties in online development.

One of the oldest and most popular client-side data storage techniques is the usage of cookies. A cookie is a tiny bit of information that a web browser saves on a user's computer after receiving it from a website. For the website to identify the user and get the stored data, the browser sends the cookie back to the server each time the user visits the website. Cookies are frequently used to store user preferences, track behavior, and authenticate users. For example, a cookie can be used to remember a user's session when they check in to a website, saving them from having to do so on future visits.

One of its main benefits is the capacity of cookies to offer a permanent storage mechanism that functions during several sessions and even after the browser has been closed. Because of their persistence, cookies are especially helpful for preserving user sessions and recording user preferences. Alternative storing methods have been developed as a result of cookies' drawbacks, which include size limitations and security issues. Cookies can only hold 4KB of data, which may not be enough to store much information. Furthermore, each HTTP request to the server includes cookies, which may result in higher latency and resource use.

Modern online browsers offer several alternative storage technologies, such as online Storage, IndexedDB, and Service Workers, to overcome the drawbacks of cookies. These storage methods provide better performance, more storage space, and more flexibility than cookies. LocalStorage and sessionStorage are Web Storage's primary storage options, first introduced in HTML5. Key-value pairs can be stored on the client side using both localStorage and sessionStorage. However, their scope and durability vary.

Even after closing and reopening the browser, data can be retained indefinitely, thanks to local storage. Because of this, localStorage is perfect for long-term data storage, including storing user preferences, application settings, and other data. For instance, a website can utilize localStorage to automatically apply the selected theme on subsequent visits by remembering the user's preferred theme (such as light or dark mode). Depending on the browser, localStorage's storage size is usually between 5 and 10 MB, far more than cookies' storage space.

Conversely, sessionStorage only keeps information for as long as the browser session is open. This implies that the data is erased when the user exits the browser window or tab. Form input values, shopping cart contents, and other transient data are examples of temporary data that can be stored using sessionStorage and are only required for the current session. SessionStorage has a comparable amount of storage as local storage, but the data is automatically deleted after the session. Because Web Storage offers local and session storage, developers can select the best storage method for their apps based on their unique needs.

The simplicity of usage of Web Storage is one of its main benefits. Simple JavaScript functions like setItem, getItem, and removeItem allow developers to work with localStorage and sessionStorage. These techniques give developers a simple and effective way to save, retrieve, and remove data. For instance, a developer can use the setItem method to save a user's name in localStorage and the getItem function to get the stored name. Because of its ease of use, online Storage is desirable for developers who want to incorporate client-side storage into their online apps.

Web storage works well for modest to moderate data storage but might not be enough for more complicated and data-intensive applications. Developers can use IndexedDB, a low-level API for client-side storing of substantial volumes of structured data, in these situations. With IndexedDB, developers may use a key-value system to store and retrieve items, offering a strong and adaptable solution for intricate data storage requirements. Applications that need strong data management features, like offline apps, progressive web apps, and data-heavy apps, are best suited for IndexedDB since they enable transactions, indexing, and querying.

Creating a database, establishing a connection, and carrying out actions like adding, retrieving, and removing data are all necessary when using IndexedDB. Because the API is asynchronous, the main thread can continue to respond while operations occur in the background. IndexedDB's asynchronous nature makes it ideal for managing huge datasets and executing intricate queries without interfering with the user interface. Even when working with large volumes of data, developers may utilize IndexedDB to create feature-rich web apps that offer a smooth and responsive user experience.

Service Workers, another contemporary storage technique, offer a means of handling and intercepting network requests, caching resources, and enabling offline functionality. Because Service Workers run in the background, developers can enhance web application speed and offer seamless offline experiences. Service Workers can lessen the need for network connectivity and guarantee that users can access content even when they are not online by intelligently managing network requests and caching resources. Additionally, Service Workers can be combined with other storage systems, such as IndexedDB, to build dependable and resilient web apps that provide a seamless and reliable user experience.

Developers must consider security and privacy concerns even though browser storage mechanisms provide strong capabilities for client-side data storage. Client-side storage of sensitive data may be vulnerable to security threats such as data theft, tampering, or illegal access. Developers should adhere to best practices, such as encrypting sensitive data, employing secure cookies, and placing appropriate access restrictions to reduce these risks. Developers should also be aware of privacy laws that control user data gathering, storing, and processing, such as the General Data Protection Regulation (GDPR). Upholding adherence to these rules is crucial to preserving user confidence and averting legal issues.

In conclusion, cookies and browser storage are essential to web development because they allow data persistence, improve user experience, and boost application speed. Although the conventional approach to client-side storage has been cookies, contemporary storage techniques like Web Storage, IndexedDB, and Service Workers provide more effective and adaptable alternatives. Developers who want to build reliable and user-friendly online apps must comprehend different storage techniques, as well as the benefits and drawbacks of each. Developers may guarantee their consumers a smooth and customized browsing experience by utilizing the appropriate storage option for every use case.

The need for effective and safe data storage solutions will only increase as web development develops further. With the emergence of offline-first tactics, data-driven apps, and progressive web apps, developers must keep up with the most recent developments in browser storage technology. Developers can produce web applications that are efficient, effective, and safe and adhere to privacy laws by becoming proficient with these technologies and adhering to best practices. By doing this, businesses will be prepared to satisfy the needs of contemporary users and provide outstanding online experiences.

The increase in mobile web usage further highlights the need for effective browser storage and cookies. Because mobile devices frequently have limited storage space and sporadic network connectivity, web applications must use robust and effective storage techniques. Developers may design mobile-friendly web apps that offer a consistent and responsive user experience across various devices and network conditions by utilizing storage solutions like localStorage, IndexedDB, and Service Workers. Reaching a wider audience and guaranteeing that consumers can easily access material, irrespective of their device or location, depend on this flexibility.

Another important consideration is the function that cookies and browser storage play in improving website performance. These techniques can minimize latency and eliminate the need for repetitive network queries by caching resources and storing data locally. A smoother user experience and quicker page loads are the outcomes of this. For instance, Service Workers can guarantee that static assets like images, stylesheets, and scripts are always accessible even when the user is not online by caching them. Similar to this, web apps can enhance efficiency and lower server load by saving user preferences and session data in localStorage rather than requiring them to be fetched from the server each time a page loads.

Cookies and browser storage allow web apps to be personalized and customized, improving performance. Web apps can customize each user's experience by saving browsing history, user preferences, and other customized information. This can involve remembering user preferences between sessions, offering tailored suggestions, and personalizing the user interface. Customization increases customer pleasure and engagement, increasing the likelihood that users will visit the website again and use the application.

Although browser storage and cookies offer numerous advantages, developers must consider these features' possible drawbacks and restrictions. One main issue is ensuring data synchronization and consistency between the client and server. Because client-side data is locally saved, there may be differences between client and server data if updates are not appropriately synchronized. Developers must implement measures to guarantee that data stays current and consistent, like resolving conflicts, utilizing synchronization algorithms, and offering tools for manual data reconciliation.

Managing various browser storage systems' restrictions and storage capacity presents another difficulty. The quantity of data that may be saved locally is still limited, even though more recent storage options have bigger storage capabilities than cookies. Developers must know these restrictions and implement plans to control storage use efficiently. Compressing data, eliminating unneeded or outdated data, and giving consumers the ability to delete stored data when necessary are a few examples of this.

Security and privacy issues are equally crucial when dealing with browser storage and cookies. Client-side storage of sensitive data exposes it to possible security risks like breaches and illegal access. Strong security measures, such as encrypting data before saving it, utilizing secure connections (HTTPS), and adhering to secure coding best practices, must be put in place by developers to safeguard stored data. Furthermore, developers have to abide by privacy laws like the GDPR.

Introduction to JavaScript Frameworks

JavaScript frameworks have transformed web development by offering scalable, organized, and effective ways to create intricate applications. These frameworks streamline the development process by providing pre-written code, reusable parts, and defined techniques for managing routine activities like data manipulation, state handling, and user interface management. JavaScript frameworks have become indispensable tools for developers aiming to construct dynamic, interactive, high-performance web applications as web applications have become more complicated. It is necessary to comprehend JavaScript frameworks' goals, advantages, major industry participants, and ways they influence contemporary web development.

A JavaScript framework is essentially an assembly of pre-written JavaScript code that serves as a basis for creating online applications. Frameworks specify an application's general structure and workflow, in contrast to JavaScript libraries, which provide particular functionality that programmers can incorporate into their applications. This implies that when developers use a framework, they adhere to a predetermined architecture that specifies how various application components should function together. This methodical approach enhances maintainability and aids in enforcing best practices, especially for large-scale projects.

Increasing productivity is one of the main reasons developers adopt JavaScript frameworks. Without a framework, developers must create repetitious code for tasks like asynchronous operations, application state management, and user interface updates. JavaScript frameworks simplify these procedures by removing needless complexity through built-in solutions. Instead of having to recreate the wheel for typical functionalities, developers can now concentrate on the distinctive features of their products. Furthermore, most frameworks have active communities and thorough documentation, facilitating learning and problem-solving during development.

The ability of JavaScript frameworks to encourage consistency and maintainability is another important advantage. Teams working on big projects can guarantee consistency in their codebase since frameworks enforce a certain structure and coding rules. This uniformity is especially helpful in collaborative settings when several developers work on the same project. Conflicting coding styles are less likely to occur in well-structured frameworks, facilitating application scaling and maintenance over time. Furthermore, frameworks frequently use modular design principles, which enhance code organization and reusability by enabling developers to divide their systems into smaller, reusable components.

Facebook created React, one of the most well-known JavaScript frameworks. React is a library for creating user interfaces rather than a complete framework. However, because its ecosystem facilitates the building of full applications and component-based architecture, it is frequently referred to as a framework. By updating only the modified portions of the user interface instead of re-rendering the entire page, React introduced the idea of a virtual DOM, which enhances performance. Because of its effectiveness, React is one of the most often used options for creating dynamic web applications. React's component-based methodology reduces redundancy and improves scalability by enabling developers to create reusable user interface elements that are simple to maintain and update.

Angular is another popular JavaScript framework that Google created. The Angular framework offers a complete set of tools for developing single-page applications. In contrast to React, which is mostly concerned with the view layer, Angular has capabilities like two-way data binding, dependency injection, and a robust templating engine. By adhering to the Model-View-Controller (MVC) or Model-View-ViewModel (MVVM) architectural patterns, angular applications enable developers to manage application logic and divide concerns effectively. Angular is a popular option for enterprise-level applications because of its integrated support for TypeScript, a statically typed JavaScript superset, improving code stability and maintainability.

Another well-liked JavaScript framework that has become widely used because of its adaptability and simplicity is Vue.js. Vue offers a lightweight yet potent solution for creating contemporary web apps by fusing the greatest features of Angular and React. Vue's component-based architecture facilitates the creation of reusable user interface elements, and its reactivity system enables effective state management. Vue is renowned for its smooth learning curve, making it a great option for novice and seasoned developers. This contrasts with Angular, which has a higher learning curve. Additionally, Vue offers a smooth connection with already-existing projects, so developers can gradually implement it instead of committing to a complete framework redesign.

A more recent JavaScript framework called Svelte approaches web application development differently. At build time, Svelte compiles components into highly efficient JavaScript, unlike React, Angular, and Vue, which depend on a virtual DOM. This improves runtime efficiency by eliminating the requirement for a virtual DOM. Svelte creates lightweight apps with minimal boilerplate code since it transfers much of the effort to the build process. Because of its creative methodology, Svelte has become a desirable choice for developers looking to create sophisticated, high-performance applications.

Many more JavaScript frameworks besides these main ones are suited to particular use cases. For instance, a React-based framework called Next.js makes server-side rendering and static site creation possible, enhancing speed and SEO. Similarly, Nuxt.js adds further functionality to Vue to enable the development of universal applications. Despite being less well-known than React or Angular, Ember.js offers a strongly held framework that adheres to rigid norms, which makes it perfect for large-scale projects that need structure and consistency.

The ability of contemporary JavaScript frameworks to make state management easier is one of its distinguishing characteristics. Taking care of data that changes over time and making sure that the user interface reflects these changes is known as managing the application state. State management is approached differently by different frameworks. For instance, Redux offers a centralized state management solution, whereas React employs hooks and the context API for local state management. Whereas Vue uses Vuex to manage application-wide data, Angular uses services and RxJS to handle reactive state. Effective state management is essential for creating scalable systems because it avoids needless re-renders and guarantees data consistency across many application components.

Additionally, JavaScript frameworks are essential for managing asynchronous tasks like retrieving data from APIs. Managing asynchronous requests and responses is handled by built-in solutions in many frameworks. While Angular offers the HttpClient module for making API calls, React handles HTTP requests using the built-in Fetch API or third-party libraries like Axios. With its integrated reactivity system, Vue provides comparable capability, enabling developers to handle asynchronous input easily. Building responsive apps that provide users with real-time updates requires efficiently handling asynchronous operations.

The ecosystem and tooling of JavaScript frameworks are also significant. Strong development tools that improve the programming experience are included with most contemporary frameworks. For instance, developers may rapidly analyze and debug their applications with the help of React Developer Tools, Angular DevTools, and Vue DevTools. Furthermore, frameworks frequently combine with package management like npm or Yarn, build tools like Vite, and module bundlers like Webpack. Automating processes like code compilation, dependency management, and hot module replacement technologies improve the efficiency of the development process.

Web development requires testing and debugging, and JavaScript frameworks offer several ways to guarantee the dependability of applications. Testing libraries like Jest, Mocha, and Cypress are supported by frameworks like React, Angular, and Vue, allowing developers to create end-to-end, integration, and unit tests. By finding errors early in the development process, automated testing lowers the possibility of problems in production and enhances code quality.

Another important factor to take into account while using JavaScript frameworks is security. Frameworks incorporate security mechanisms to reduce the risks associated with web applications, which are vulnerable to attacks like cross-site scripting (XSS) and cross-site request forgery (CSRF). Angular, for example, automatically sanitizes input data to provide built-in security against XSS attacks. Best practices include utilizing secure authentication techniques and escaping user input are encouraged by React and Vue. Maintaining user confidence and safeguarding sensitive data when utilizing JavaScript frameworks requires security precautions.

As new techniques and technologies are developed, JavaScript frameworks will continue to change. Frameworks are evolving to satisfy the growing needs of contemporary web development as serverless architectures, static site creation, and progressive web apps gain traction. Innovations like React's concurrent rendering evidence the continuous development of these frameworks, Svelte's better compiler optimizations, and Vue 3's modular improvements.

To summarize, JavaScript frameworks have revolutionized online application development by offering organized approaches to managing user interfaces, state management, asynchronous processes, and performance enhancement. Among the most popular frameworks are React, Angular, Vue, and Svelte; each has special benefits appropriate for certain development requirements. Utilizing JavaScript frameworks has several advantages, such as increased security, performance, maintainability, and productivity. As the online development environment changes, JavaScript frameworks will continue to be crucial resources for creating scalable and effective apps. Any developer hoping to build cutting-edge web applications that satisfy the needs of the new digital world must be aware of their capabilities and best practices.

Animations and Interactivity

In contemporary web development, animations and interactivity are essential components that improve user experience by making websites more visually appealing, intuitive, and engaging. Developers may produce immersive digital experiences that react dynamically to user activities by combining animations and interaction. This makes programs feel more responsive, guides users through the material, and provides feedback. Animations have progressed from straightforward transitions to intricate, physics-based movements due to the development of strong front-end technology, and interactivity has improved so users may interact with web content in increasingly meaningful ways.

Although the idea of online animation has existed since the beginning of the internet, it has made tremendous strides since the creation of contemporary CSS,

JavaScript, and web APIs. At first, animated GIFs and Flash-based components were mostly used to create animations, which had drawbacks in terms of accessibility and performance. Web animation has been transformed with the advent of CSS animations and JavaScript-based solutions, which enable more fluid, effective, and adaptable motion effects. Depending on the use case, many technologies, such as CSS animations, CSS transitions, JavaScript, SVG animations, and WebGL, are used to create animations nowadays. Each of these technologies has advantages of its own.

Without using JavaScript, CSS animations and transitions offer a straightforward but effective method of producing motion effects. Transitions enable components to change characteristics smoothly over a predetermined period when a state changes, such as a hover or click event. For instance, a transition can change a button's background color as it is hovered over, improving the interaction's visual attractiveness. Conversely, more intricate animations are made possible via CSS animations, which define keyframes that specify various states of an element over time. Because CSS animations are intended for hardware acceleration, developers may easily and efficiently construct dynamic visual upgrades like fading effects, sliding motions, and looping animations.

Because JavaScript enables developers to modify DOM elements in response to user input dynamically, it offers much more freedom for producing animations and interactive elements. JavaScript-based animations allow developers to design sophisticated interactions, coordinate animations with user actions, and manage animations programmatically, unlike CSS animations, which are predetermined and have a limited scope. For producing high-performance animations with sophisticated features like easing, timelines, and physics-based motion, libraries like anime.js and GSAP (GreenSock Animation Platform) have gained popularity.

These libraries are perfect for producing rich, dynamic experiences because they offer powerful capabilities for animating HTML, SVG, and Canvas elements.

SVG animations are another effective method for making pictures come to life on the web. Developers can use CSS, JavaScript, or the SVG animate element to generate resolution-independent pictures with Scalable Vector Graphics (SVG). SVG animations are especially helpful when making dynamic icons, loading spinners, data visualizations, and other graphical effects that need to scale smoothly without sacrificing quality. Since SVG elements are a component of the DOM, JavaScript can be used to change them dynamically, opening up countless possibilities for creating complex UI elements, animated infographics, and interactive artwork.

WebGL and the Canvas API make real-time graphics rendering and intricate visual effects possible, pushing the limits of online animations. With the help of WebGL, a JavaScript API for rendering 2D and 3D graphics, developers can use GPU acceleration to produce dynamic experiences and high-performance animations. Applications requiring high frame rates and sophisticated rendering techniques, such as virtual reality, gaming, and interactive data visualization, use this technology extensively. Another strong animation tool is the Canvas API, which gives developers a working surface for dynamic visuals and enables programmable pixel manipulation and drawing. These technologies allow the development of visually stunning and immersive applications beyond conventional web design.

Animations and interactivity go hand in hand in web development since user interactions frequently result in motion effects that improve the user experience. By offering simple navigation and feedback, interactive features like buttons, menus, carousels, and modal windows enhance usability. JavaScript is essential for managing user interactions by utilizing event listeners to identify keystrokes, mouse movements, clicks, and touch gestures. Developers can design dynamic, responsive interfaces by reacting to user input in real-time.

Hover effects, which give users visual feedback when interacting with objects, are among the most prevalent interactive features in contemporary web applications. Simple hover effects like altering a button's color or more intricate ones like launching animations that disclose buried content are possible. These effects improve usability by highlighting which items are interactive and how they react to user inputs. Hover-based animations work especially well in call-to-action buttons, picture galleries, and navigation menus, where minor motion can increase engagement.

Scrolling animations have gained popularity in web design because they offer a dynamic method of revealing material as users scroll down a page. This method, called parallax scrolling, moves the foreground and background items at varying speeds to provide the impression of depth. Implementing scroll-based animations is made simple by JavaScript libraries like ScrollMagic and Locomotive Scroll, which let programmers activate effects like text fading, graphic animation, and section revelation based on scroll position. Websites feel more immersive and engaging when scrolling animations are used to improve storytelling and visually guide users through content.

Another interactive feature that enhances the user experience is drag-and-drop functionality, which lets users move objects about the screen. Applications like file uploads, interactive games, and task management software frequently leverage this feature. Through the HTML5 Drag and Drop API, JavaScript offers built-in support for drag-and-drop interactions, allowing programmers to design user-friendly interfaces that will enable users to sort lists, rearrange things, and interact with elements naturally. These interactions seem smooth and fulfilling due to drag-and-drop animations, improving their visual attractiveness.

Microinteractions are tiny, nuanced animations that enhance usability and offer feedback. These consist of effects like notification popups, loading spinners, form validation indicators, and button clicks. Despite their seemingly insignificant appearance, micro-interactions are essential for improving the user experience overall since they provide programs with a more polished and responsive feel. Clear visual cues and reinforcement of user actions are two ways that well-designed micro-interactions can increase usability and engagement.

An emerging trend in web design is interactive storytelling, which uses animations and interactivity to lead people through a tale. Animations dynamically expose content on websites that use interactive storytelling, making the user experience more engaging. This method is frequently employed in e-learning platforms, digital marketing, and journalism, where captivating images and motion effects improve the narrative. Developers may produce gripping stories that captivate users and promote exploration by fusing animations with user-driven interactions.

To ensure that all users, including those with impairments, can properly interact with web information, web animations, and interactivity are also crucial. Accessibility should be considered when creating animations so that users who depend on assistive technology have options. Avoiding excessive motion that can be uncomfortable for users with vestibular problems and offering the option to stop animations if necessary are two recommendations made by the Web Content Accessibility Guidelines (WCAG). Web applications become more inclusive when interactive parts are accessible to all users through ARIA characteristics, keyboard navigation support, and semantic HTML.

Because badly optimized animations can affect responsiveness and page load times, performance optimization is crucial to animations and interactivity. By shifting rendering duties to the graphics processor, hardware-accelerated animations, like those that use CSS transforms and the GPU-optimized will-change property, contribute to increased efficiency. An improved user experience can be achieved by reducing the number of pointless reflows and repaints, cutting down on JavaScript execution time, and utilizing request AnimationFrame to create fluid animations. To guarantee seamless performance across various screen sizes and hardware capabilities, developers should test animations on several devices and browsers.

As technology advances, animations and interaction in web development will continue to change. Artificial intelligence (AI) and machine learning in interactive experiences make personalized animations and adaptive interfaces possible. AI-powered animations may react to real-time user inputs, resulting in more intelligent and contextually aware interactions. Augmented reality (AR) and virtual reality (VR) offer new user engagement methods by enabling users to interact with digital content in immersive settings. The importance of animations and interaction in producing captivating, user-friendly digital experiences will only increase as web technologies advance.

Modern web development requires animations and interactivity to improve usability, aesthetics, and user engagement. With today's technologies and approaches, developers can create dynamic online experiences in countless ways, from basic transitions to intricate 3D animations. Developers can develop captivating websites and applications with smooth, user-friendly interactions using CSS animations, JavaScript libraries, SVG, WebGL, and interactive design principles. Future developments in web animation and interactivity offer even more creative and immersive experiences as technology advances, influencing how people engage with digital information in novel and fascinating ways.

Building a Simple JavaScript Project

Developing a basic JavaScript project is a great method to improve your programming abilities, comprehend fundamental ideas, and obtain real-world web development experience. JavaScript is one of the most popular programming languages for making dynamic, interactive websites. With a straightforward project, developers can practice basic JavaScript concepts, including variables, functions, loops, event handling, and the Document Object Model. Building a project from the ground up teaches developers how to organize their code, troubleshoot problems, and sharpen their problem-solving abilities. Such a project's experience is a strong basis for future, more intricate web applications.

The first step in developing a JavaScript project is to plan its functionality and scope. It is crucial to have a clear idea of what the project is supposed to achieve before creating any code. A roadmap for implementation can be made by outlining the features, user interactions, and intended behavior. Usually, a basic JavaScript project includes user input, dynamic content changes, and web page interactions. Setting a goal for the project is essential to keeping it focused and reasonable, especially for novices still learning how to program. Planning guarantees a seamless development process for any project, be it an interactive quiz, weather app, to-do list, or basic calculator.

Setting up the development environment comes next after the project idea is complete. An HTML file for the webpage layout, a CSS file for styling, and a JavaScript file for functionality comprise the fundamental framework needed for a JavaScript project. Code editors like Visual Studio Code and Sublime Text increase productivity by offering syntax highlighting, debugging tools, and code suggestions. A neat and orderly project is easier to navigate and update when files are appropriately organized. Early workflow establishment results in better coding techniques and increased productivity in subsequent projects.

Building any project requires an understanding of how JavaScript interacts with the webpage. JavaScript uses the Document Object Model to alter items on a webpage. The DOM represents a web page's structure, a tree of elements that JavaScript may access and change. Developers can manage user interactions, alter styles, and dynamically update content by choosing items using techniques like querySelector. Thanks to event listeners, JavaScript can react to user actions like button clicks, form submissions, and keyboard inputs. Integrating event-driven programming can create real-time interactive features that respond to user actions.

An essential component of many JavaScript projects is handling user input. JavaScript offers several ways to gather and handle user input, whether for tracking button clicks, recognizing keyboard events, or extracting text from a form. Verifying user input reduces the possibility of mistakes or security threats and guarantees that the data entered is correct. User experience is enhanced, and unwanted behavior is avoided with basic validation methods, including displaying error warnings, verifying proper formats, and checking for empty fields. Developers improve the dependability and usefulness of their products by incorporating input processing and validation.

Another essential component of JavaScript projects is the ability to update content dynamically. JavaScript enables modifications to be made immediately to the webpage based on user interactions, eliminating the need for a page refresh. A smooth and interesting user experience is enhanced by dynamically changing styles, showing messages, updating text, and adjusting visibility. Real-time element manipulation with JavaScript gives web apps a responsive, dynamic feel. Knowledge about effectively updating the DOM without needless re-renders enhances performance and guarantees seamless transitions.

Logic and control flow must be incorporated to add functionality to a JavaScript project. Using conditional statements, developers can define distinct behaviors depending on user actions or data conditions. Loops make it possible to perform repetitive activities like creating lists, iterating through data, and effectively processing many components. By dividing tasks into reusable chunks, functions aid in code organization, making the project modular and simpler to manage. Code that is organized using functions and logical control is easier to read and debug.

The development process will inevitably involve debugging, and learning how to spot and correct mistakes is essential. Syntax issues, faulty logic, or unexpected user input can all result in JavaScript failures. When using browser developer tools, it is easier to examine elements, monitor events, and examine console error messages. Insights into variable values and execution flow can be obtained by inserting console.log statements at strategic locations throughout the code. Knowledge of popular debugging approaches improves problem-solving abilities and expedites troubleshooting. Writing clear, well-commented code also makes it easier to spot problems early on and keep the project's focus.

Using CSS to improve a JavaScript project's visual appeal enhances user engagement and experience. Applying responsive design concepts, integrating animations, and styling components enhances the project's usability and aesthetic appeal on various devices. Pre-made components from CSS frameworks like Bootstrap expedite the styling process and guarantee layout uniformity. Dynamic visual effects, including color changes, hover effects, and seamless transitions, are made possible by combining JavaScript and CSS. The project's overall quality is raised by designing an aesthetically beautiful interface.

Local storage capabilities enhance the utility of a JavaScript project by enabling data to persist across page reloads. Local storage offers a means to save settings, save progress, and keep user preferences without using a backend database. JavaScript's local storage API makes it simple for developers to store and retrieve modest quantities of data. This capability greatly benefits applications like note-taking apps, to-do lists, and settings customizations. Adding local storage enhances the functionality of basic JavaScript projects and gives consumers a more customized experience.

Thorough testing of the project guarantees that it satisfies user expectations and operates as intended. Testing entails confirming predicted results, validating input handling, and examining every potential user interaction. Potential errors or inconsistencies can be found by identifying edge cases and testing various scenarios. Getting input from users or other developers offers important information about usability and potential areas for development. The project's performance and stability are improved via ongoing testing and improvement.

When the project is deployed, users can access it, and developers can display their work. JavaScript projects can be published online for free and easily using hosting services like GitHub Pages, Netlify, or Vercel. Collaboration and version control are made possible by uploading the project to a code repository, which facilitates tracking modifications and update management. Giving the project to others lets you show off your coding abilities, get feedback, and develop a portfolio. Project maintenance and publication offer hands-on experience with real-world development processes.

After finishing a basic JavaScript project, adding more features and enhancements is a logical next step. Enhancing performance, improving logic, and adding new features facilitate the progression from simple projects to more complex applications. A project can be further enhanced by adding animations for a better user experience, integrating real-time data APIs, or establishing user account authentication. Growing as a developer is facilitated by consistently learning new JavaScript concepts and trying various approaches.

Constructing a basic JavaScript project is a priceless educational opportunity that strengthens problem-solving and programming principles. Every stage of the process, from organizing and designing the project to putting functionality in place and launching it online, offers practical web development experience. The basis for more complex projects is understanding how JavaScript works with the DOM, manages user input, and dynamically updates content. Testing, debugging, and project refinement increase coding productivity and guarantee a high-caliber product. By continuously creating and growing projects, developers boost their self-esteem, sharpen their abilities, and become ready for future, more complicated applications.

CHAPTER VI

Advanced JavaScript Concepts

Object-Oriented Programming (OOP) in JavaScript

JavaScript's Object-Oriented Programming (OOP) paradigm is essential for developers to effectively organize and manage code, increasing its scalability, reusability, and maintainability. OOP, in contrast to conventional procedural programming, is based on the idea of objects, which are containers for information and actions. Because JavaScript is a dynamic and versatile language, it supports OOP concepts through ES6 classes and prototypes, enabling developers to create intricate applications with organized code.

The four main tenets of OOP are abstraction, polymorphism, inheritance, and encapsulation. Encapsulating data and actions inside an object to prevent direct access and guarantee data integrity is known as encapsulation. This is accomplished in JavaScript using ES6 class syntax with private fields, closures, and private variables. Encapsulation safeguards an object's internal state by restricting external access to specific properties, which lowers the likelihood of unintentional changes and increases code maintainability.

Another essential component of OOP that allows objects to inherit methods and properties from a parent class is inheritance. This lessens repetition and encourages code reuse. In JavaScript, inheritance is implemented through prototype chaining in previous versions or the extends keyword in ES6 classes. Developers can improve the code structure and minimize repetition by using inheritance to establish hierarchical relationships between objects. For instance, certain courses, such as Dogs and Cats, can extend a base class that represents the generic Animal by adding unique behaviors and inheriting common characteristics.

Because of polymorphism, objects can behave differently while still being regarded as instances of their parent class. This is especially helpful when various classes implement methods differently but have a common interface. Method overriding, in which a subclass redefines a method inherited from its parent class, is how JavaScript accomplishes polymorphism. This increases the flexibility of the code by enabling functions to handle various object types without the need for explicit type checking.

The approach of presenting only the essential functionality while concealing intricate implementation details is known as abstraction. It makes coding simpler by hiding the underlying logic and offering obvious interfaces for interaction. JavaScript does abstraction through abstract patterns in interfaces, ES6 classes, and constructor methods. Code becomes cleaner and easier to manage as a result of developers being able to concentrate on high-level functionality rather than internal intricacies.

There are several ways to generate objects in JavaScript, such as ES6 classes, constructor functions, and object literals. The most straightforward method of defining objects with key-value pairs is through object literals. Nevertheless, this method cannot be reused to create numerous instances with the same characteristics. Using the new keyword, constructor functions—popular before ES6—offer a reusable method of producing multiple object instances. They allow method declaration on the prototype to save memory while facilitating object instantiation and property initialization.

The class syntax was introduced with ES6 to give JavaScript programmers a better organized and user-friendly method of implementing OOP. ES6 classes preserve backward compatibility with prototype-based inheritance while streamlining object creation, inheritance, and method design. While methods can be defined inside the class body, a constructor method initializes object properties. To facilitate smooth inheritance, the super keyword grants access to the constructor and methods of the parent class.

JavaScript's OOP model is based on object prototypes, which it supports. In JavaScript, each object has an internal prototype that connects to another object to form a chain of prototypes. Through this process, objects can inherit methods and properties from their prototype, allowing for more efficient memory use. Reducing repetition and encouraging code reuse, the Object.new() method offers a means to generate objects using a specified prototype.

Mixins, which enable objects to share functionality without traditional inheritance, are another key idea in JavaScript OOP. Mixins help combine several behaviors into one object, encouraging code reuse and modularity. Developers can use mixins and JavaScript's Object.assign() method or distributing properties to increase object capabilities.

Closures and the # sign for private fields in ES6 classes are further ways to improve encapsulation in JavaScript. Closures allow functions to construct private data while maintaining access to variables from their outer scope. A more formal method of declaring private attributes inside a class, private fields, was introduced in ES2020, limiting direct access outside the class.

Effective modeling of real-world entities is one of the main benefits of utilizing OOP in JavaScript. Developers can produce modular and reusable components that improve maintainability by employing objects to organize code. Thanks to OOP concepts, complex programs can be better organized, making scaling, extending, and debugging projects simpler. Additionally, classes and inheritance streamline the development process by encouraging uniformity and minimizing code duplication.

However, the OOP methodology of JavaScript is distinct from that of conventional class-based languages like Java and C++. JavaScript primarily uses a prototype-based model, even though it allows class syntax. This distinction makes More flexibility possible, but developers must comprehend prototype inheritance and its ramifications. In contrast to rigorously typed OOP languages, JavaScript's dynamic nature enables objects to be changed at runtime, providing strong but possibly dangerous behavior if improperly handled.

Modern frameworks and libraries like React, Angular, and Vue.js extensively use JavaScript's OOP. These frameworks use OOP concepts to manage the state efficiently, produce reusable components, and support organized application development. For example, components in React are frequently defined as functions or classes, encapsulating states, and logic in reusable modules. This improves maintainability and scalability and is consistent with OOP's objective of modularity and abstraction.

JavaScript OOP also takes performance into account. Although code organization is enhanced by object-oriented structures, overuse of classes and inheritance can result in needless complexity and performance overhead. Developers must balance OOP concepts and performance optimization to keep code effective and maintainable. Optimizing prototype chain lookups, utilizing object pooling for memory efficiency, and prioritizing composition over inheritance are best practices that improve JavaScript application speed.

Tools and techniques compatible with JavaScript OOP code's dynamic nature are necessary for debugging and testing it. Debugging tools offered by contemporary programming environments enable developers to examine class structures, prototype chains, and object characteristics. Automated testing of object-oriented programming is made easier by unit testing frameworks like Jest and Mocha, which guarantee accuracy and dependability.

In JavaScript OOP, security considerations are equally crucial. Although encapsulation prevents accidental data alteration, developers must exercise caution when disclosing private information. Limiting direct data modification, private fields, closures, and getters and setters for controlled property access improves security. Additionally, security concerns in JavaScript applications are reduced by following secure coding principles, such as input validation and refraining from global object change.

New features and improvements in OOP further increase development efficiency as JavaScript develops. The possibilities of JavaScript's object-oriented methodology are improved by adding decorators, class fields, and enhanced module systems. Developers may anticipate more reliable tools and techniques to simplify OOP in JavaScript as it evolves, increasing its functionality and accessibility.

To sum up, JavaScript's Object-Oriented Programming offers an organized and effective method for creating modular, scalable, and maintainable programs. Developers can build complicated systems while preserving the readability and reusability of their code by utilizing encapsulation, inheritance, polymorphism, and abstraction. With the help of ES6 classes and JavaScript's distinctive prototype-based paradigm, OOP concepts may be implemented flexibly and strongly. Modern web development requires an understanding of and ability to use OOP in JavaScript, which makes it possible to create dynamic, effective, and well-structured apps. Keeping up with the most recent OOP approaches and best practices as the language develops guarantees that developers may fully utilize JavaScript to create complex and effective software solutions.

JavaScript Modules and Import/Export

In contemporary web development, JavaScript modules have completely transformed how developers organize and handle code. Keeping a well-structured codebase becomes crucial as web apps get more complicated. Large applications can be divided into smaller, reusable components using JavaScript modules, which improves code's scalability, maintainability, and debugging. Global variables, Immediately Invoked Function Expressions (IIFE), and CommonJS, used in Node.js, were replaced by the ES6 module system, often known as ES modules (ESM), which standardized how JavaScript handles modularity. Modern programming requires understanding JavaScript modules and import/export techniques, especially in back-end systems like Node.js and front-end frameworks like React, Vue, and Angular.

The concepts of encapsulation and reusability are fundamental to JavaScript modules. Developers can produce modular files, each module containing only the code required for a particular purpose, as an alternative to writing a monolithic script with all functions and variables existing in the global scope. This method allows developers to reuse functions, classes, or variables across several files without writing duplicate code, avoid name conflicts, and enhance readability. Better separation of concerns is made possible by the modular system, a cornerstone of software engineering. Code is arranged into separate files so developers can quickly find and change particular features without affecting other application portions.

JavaScript did not have an integrated module system prior to the release of ES modules. The Module Pattern, which simulated private and public scopes using closures, was one of the remedies that developers turned to. Another popular strategy was the CommonJS module system, which started in Node.js and let developers import other modules via the `require()` method. However, because CommonJS was created for server-side JavaScript, it proved ineffective for client-side applications that require asynchronous loading due to its synchronous nature. Similar to this, AMD (Asynchronous Module Definition) added complexity while offering a means of loading modules asynchronously through the use of `define()` and `require()`. By providing a uniform syntax that functions in both browsers and contemporary JavaScript environments, ES6 modules overcame these drawbacks.

`Import` and `export` are the two main keywords that form the foundation of the ES module system. Developers can specify which functions, variables, or classes should be available from other files using the `export` keyword, and other modules can use these exported parts by using the `import` keyword. The code is clearer, and accidental changes to global variables are avoided thanks to this explicit disclosure of dependencies. Named and default exports are the two main methods for exporting values from a module. When several functions or constants need to be shared, named exports offer flexibility by enabling the export of multiple values from a module. In contrast, default exports are used when a module should only export one primary value. This makes it easier to import without the need for particular identifiers.

By enabling developers to import only the components that are required, named exports promote modularity by cutting down on pointless code execution and enhancing efficiency. This is especially helpful in large-scale applications where many modules may share some features but not others. However, default exports are advantageous when a module represents a single thing, like a configuration object or a utility function. The project structure and preferred coding style will determine whether to use named or default exports.

The capability of ES modules to facilitate static analysis is one of their benefits. JavaScript engines may examine module dependencies at build time since the import and export statements are declarative and must be positioned at the module's top level. This makes tree shaking, which bundlers like Webpack and Rollup employ to remove unnecessary code from the output possible. By making JavaScript bundles smaller, tree shaking speeds up load times and enhances application performance. ES modules provide more effective optimizations than CommonJS, which resolves module dependencies dynamically at runtime.

Asynchronous browser loading of JavaScript modules is essential for enhancing page performance. Browsers automatically delay the execution of ES modules when they are used in HTML via `<script type="module">`; that is, they are loaded after the HTML content has been parsed. By doing this, extra `defer` or `async` characteristics are not required, increasing the predictability of script loading. Another feature ES modules provide is module federation, which enables modules to be loaded dynamically at runtime instead of being packaged into a single file. This method is especially helpful for micro-frontends, where many teams can create separate modules that are dynamically integrated.

JavaScript modules can be used for more than only front-end development. ES modules substitute for CommonJS in Node.js, enabling programmers to utilize the `import` and `export` syntax in server-side applications. However, due to backward compatibility issues, Node.js has traditionally depended on CommonJS as its preferred module system. Developers must use `.mjs` file extensions or specify the `type` field in `package.json` to `"module to use ES modules with Node.js. Better consistency with contemporary JavaScript syntax and enhanced interoperability with front-end codebases are two advantages of switching from CommonJS to ES modules in Node.js.

JavaScript modules provide certain difficulties despite their benefits, especially compatibility and performance. Developers must ensure their code adheres to best practices, such as avoiding undeclared variables and utilizing appropriate scoping because ES modules employ strict mode by default. Furthermore, not all browsers—especially earlier versions of Internet Explorer—fully support ES modules. Developers frequently utilize build tools like Babel to translate the syntax of ES modules into backward-compatible formats to fix compatibility issues. By bundling several modules into a single optimized file, module bundlers such as Webpack, Parcel, and Rollup improve compatibility by lowering the quantity of HTTP requests required to load an application.

Managing dependencies is another issue with JavaScript modules. Managing multiple dependencies is often necessary for large-scale applications, and poor management might result in conflicts over module resolution. Package dependencies may be effectively managed with tools like npm and yarn. Still, developers need to be aware of versioning problems when various modules depend on different versions of the same package. Package managers employ lock files as a countermeasure to guarantee that versions are installed consistently across development environments.

Another useful feature of JavaScript modules is dynamic imports. With dynamic imports, modules can be loaded conditionally using the `import()` function, which is resolved at compile time, unlike static imports. By enabling lazy loading, which loads modules only when necessary, this feature enhances the speed at which pages load initially. Large applications where not all components must be loaded at once benefit greatly from lazy loading. For instance, a single-page application can reduce the initial bundle size and improve user experience by using dynamic imports to load specific features only when users browse particular routes.

Additionally, better testing and debugging procedures are made possible by JavaScript modules. Writing unit tests is made easier by modules, which divide functionality into smaller pieces. To ensure that tests execute consistently, developers can isolate dependencies and mimic module imports using testing frameworks like Jest, Mocha, and Jasmine. Additionally, developers may more efficiently track execution flow and examine module dependencies thanks to improved debugging capabilities offered by contemporary browsers.

Another crucial component of JavaScript modules is security. Developers can limit access to private information and avoid unintentional changes to vital features by encapsulating code into modules. Additionally, modules enforce the least privilege principle, which states that an application's components should only have access to the required resources. To reduce potential vulnerabilities, developers must still adhere to recommended security practices, which include verifying input data, avoiding eval-based imports, and maintaining up-to-date dependencies.

JavaScript module usage has greatly impacted contemporary web development frameworks and libraries. Developers are encouraged to divide apps into reusable components by frameworks like React, Angular, and Vue, which mostly rely on modular architecture. This modular approach improves team communication because several developers can work on distinct modules independently. Further illustrating the adaptability of JavaScript modules, server-side rendering frameworks such as Next.js use ES modules to maximize scalability and performance.

As new standards and best practices emerge, JavaScript modules will continue to change. By adding new features like built-in module caching, better interoperability with CommonJS, and increased support for web assembly modules, initiatives like the ESNext proposals seek to expand module capabilities. JavaScript modules will continue to be essential to effective and maintainable development as the online ecosystem develops, guaranteeing that applications may grow while preserving security and performance.

To sum up, JavaScript modules and the import/export mechanism have completely changed how programmers organize and handle code. Modules offer a scalable approach to modern web application development by encouraging encapsulation, reusability, and maintainability. Many of the drawbacks of earlier modular systems have been fixed by standardizing ES modules, allowing for enhanced compatibility, smoother integration with front-end and back-end technologies, and greater performance optimizations. Although there are still issues with browser compatibility and dependency management, the advantages of modular programming greatly exceed these drawbacks. Modules will continue to be a crucial tool for developers looking to create effective, scalable, and maintainable programs in a digital environment that is becoming more complex as JavaScript develops.

Functional Programming in JavaScript

JavaScript's functional programming paradigm avoids mutable data and changing states by treating computation as evaluating mathematical functions.

JavaScript is an effective tool for creating modular, reusable, and manageable code because its foundational principles prioritize immutability, pure functions, and first-class functions. Although JavaScript has always been regarded as a multi-paradigm language that supports procedural and object-oriented programming methods, its functional programming features have become increasingly significant as contemporary web development has advanced.

Using pure functions—functions that never cause side effects and always return the same output given the same input—is the fundamental idea behind functional programming. Any operation that alters the state outside the function's scope is referred to as having side effects. Examples of such operations include updating a data structure, a global variable, or input/output operations. Functional programming facilitates code reasoning by removing side effects, resulting in more reliable and error-proof applications. Debugging and testing become much easier when functions only work on their inputs and return outputs without changing external states.

Immutability is another essential tenet of functional programming, which states that it should not be altered once data is produced. Functional programming promotes the generation of new data structures with the needed adjustments rather than altering pre-existing ones. This method lessens the difficulty of monitoring state changes and avoids unexpected adverse effects. In concurrent programming, immutability is very useful since it removes race problems and unpredictable behavior brought on by changes to the shared state. Working with immutable data allows developers to create applications that are easier to grow and manage, more dependable, and consistent.

JavaScript's first-class functions, which enable functions to be viewed as values, are a crucial component of functional programming. As a result, functions can be returned from functions, set to variables, and supplied as arguments to other functions. Higher-order functions—functions that take other functions as parameters or return them as results—are made possible by this feature. Because higher-order functions enable programmers to design general, abstract functions that may be used in various contexts without repeating logic, they improve the reusability and composability of code. This results in code that is easier to extend and maintain and is more expressive and modular.

Another potent idea in functional programming is function composition, which combines smaller functions to create larger, more intricate ones. Function composition promotes decomposing logic into smaller, reusable functions that may be chained together rather than creating monolithic functions that carry out numerous tasks. By isolating concerns and guaranteeing that each function has a single duty, this modular approach enhances the readability and maintainability of code. Composability enables programmers to create scalable and adaptable systems by repurposing pre-existing routines to address novel issues.

Declarative programming, which emphasizes outlining what should be done rather than how, is a fundamental component of functional programming. In contrast, imperative programming involves developers explicitly defining every computation step. By abstracting away low-level implementation details and expressing logic in a clearer, more legible way, declarative programming makes code simpler. The usage of built-in JavaScript techniques like map, filter, and reduce—which let developers handle and transform data declaratively—is encouraged by functional programming. By wrapping iteration logic into higher-order functions, these approaches work with arrays and offer a sophisticated substitute for conventional loops.

A common method in functional programming as an alternative to loops is recursion. Until a base condition is satisfied, a recursion function calls itself with a changed input. This method works especially well to tackle problems involving nested or hierarchical structures, such as tree traversal and mathematical calculations. By avoiding variable reassignment and mutable loop counters, recursion encourages immutability and brings code closer to functional programming concepts. Tail call optimization can help reduce stack overflow issues by making too many function calls, but it must be handled carefully.

Because they allow functions to preserve state without depending on global variables, closures are important in functional programming. When an inner function maintains access to variables from its outer function after the outer function has completed running, this is known as a closure. This makes code cleaner and more secure by enabling developers to encapsulate data and create private scopes. Closures are useful for managing the state while upholding immutability and function purity. They are frequently used in functional programming to build function factories, data hiding, and event handling.

Another functional programming method is currying, which turns a function with several arguments into tasks that only accept one argument each. Partial application is made possible by this method, in which certain arguments are supplied beforehand and some later. Currying improves code reusability by enabling programmers to construct specialized functions from a more general function. This strategy enhances modularity and reduces redundancy, making it especially helpful when functions must be dynamically changed based on context.

A functional programming approach, "lazy evaluation," postpones a function's execution until the desired outcome is required. This method maximizes performance by avoiding pointless calculations and memory utilization. Generators and iterators are two JavaScript mechanisms that enable lazy evaluation by allowing calculations to be interrupted and resumed as needed. Large dataset processing, data streaming, and performance optimization in resource-intensive applications are all aided by lazy evaluation.

Referential transparency, which allows a function to be substituted with its result without changing its behavior, is another benefit of functional programming. This characteristic makes testing and optimizing functions simpler by guaranteeing that they perform consistently and yield predictable results. Referential transparency enhances code maintainability by lowering reliance on external states and eliminates the need for intricate debugging. Developers can create code that is safer, more reliable, and simpler to understand by following this principle.

The advantages of functional programming in JavaScript for creating scalable and maintainable applications have led to its widespread adoption. Functional programming ideas are used by several contemporary JavaScript frameworks and libraries, like React and Redux, to manage state and application logic effectively. For instance, React promotes predictability and reusability by encouraging the usage of pure functions in component rendering. Redux is a state management library that updates the state using pure reducer functions and enforces immutability, aspects of functional programming.

Additionally, functional programming is essential to JavaScript server-side development. Functional programming approaches are supported by Node.js, a well-liked runtime environment for creating scalable network applications, to manage event-driven architectures and handle asynchronous processes. With functional programming, programmers may create non-blocking code that handles concurrent requests more effectively and efficiently by utilizing higher-order functions, promises, and async/awaits.

JavaScript functional programming includes many drawbacks and compromises despite its benefits. Because new objects and data structures must be created rather than modified, the emphasis on immutability and pure functions can occasionally result in higher memory consumption. Additionally, there is a learning curve for functional programming, especially for developers used to imperative or object-oriented paradigms. Though they may necessitate a mental shift, concepts like recursion, closures, and higher-order functions offer strong tools for creating clearer and easier-to-maintain code.

Debugging and speed optimization are additional factors to consider when functional programming. Stack traces can become complicated due to functional programming's heavy reliance on function composition and higher-order functions, which makes problem identification more difficult. Furthermore, deep recursion, many function calls, and the construction of intermediate data structures can affect performance if not effectively controlled. These issues are lessened by optimizations like lazy evaluation, memoization, and tail call optimization, which guarantee that functional programming is still effective in practical applications.

Functional programming in JavaScript is becoming increasingly popular, and new language features and tools support its tenets. Functional programming is now more approachable and expressive thanks to improvements like arrow functions, spread operators, and the const keyword introduced with ES6 and later versions. Utility functions provided by libraries like Ramda and Lodash enable developers to build elegant and succinct code by facilitating functional programming techniques.

Functional programming's growing popularity emphasizes how crucial it is to contemporary software development and how it may enhance the quality and maintainability of programs.

JavaScript functional programming provides a strong and effective way to create scalable, modular, and clean programs. Functional programming improves code's readability, maintainability, and reusability by focusing on declarative programming, pure functions, immutability, and first-class functions. Functional programming is a useful tool for developers looking to create reliable and effective programs since, despite some difficulties in implementing this paradigm, the advantages exceed the disadvantages. Functional programming concepts will continue to be a cornerstone of contemporary web development as JavaScript develops further, influencing how programmers create and execute software solutions.

Performance Optimization and Best Practices

Performance optimization is a crucial component of any system, whether it concerns software development, corporate procedures, or even individual productivity. Optimization aims to increase effectiveness, decrease resource consumption, and boost efficiency. Performance optimization is more crucial than ever in today's fast-paced world when competitive marketplaces and technology breakthroughs require greater efficiency. Finding inefficiencies and putting best practices into place can result in significant gains, whether the process is computer programs, manufacturing processes, or organizational workflows.

Finding bottlenecks is one of the core ideas of performance improvement. Bottlenecks happen when a system's overall performance is limited by one component, leading to delays and inefficiencies. For instance, inefficient code, subpar database queries, or high memory usage can all lead to bottlenecks in software development. Bottlenecks in company operations may result from ineffective resource allocation, antiquated technology, or sluggish decision-making procedures. Optimizing performance begins with a thorough system analysis, identifying the precise areas that require improvement using process mapping techniques or profiling tools. Targeted measures can be used to alleviate bottlenecks once they have been identified.

Resource management is another essential component of performance optimization. Optimizing the use of computer power, memory, time, and personnel is ensured by effective resource management. This could include caching techniques, load balancing, or memory allocation algorithms in computers. On the other hand, companies may prioritize effective logistics, appropriate scheduling, and worker productivity. An optimized system guarantees that no resources are wasted and that every part functions as a whole. For example, auto-scaling techniques assist in dynamically allocating resources according to demand in cloud computing environments, avoiding resource excess and underuse. Similarly, prioritization frameworks like the Eisenhower Matrix or Agile techniques aid in time and effort optimization in project management by prioritizing high-value tasks first.

Continuous monitoring and assessment are also necessary for performance optimization. What is deemed optimum today could not be efficient tomorrow since systems change over time. Maintaining optimal performance is aided by regular data analysis, feedback loops, and performance audits. Software engineers may track real-time performance indicators and adjust using technologies like benchmarking, automated testing, and performance monitoring dashboards. Key performance indicators (KPIs) are another tool businesses may use to monitor efficiency and modify their plans. Even the best-optimized system may deteriorate over time due to shifting needs and outside influences if it is not continuously assessed.

Enhancing scalability is another essential optimization component. In addition to operating effectively in the present, a well-optimized system should be able to manage rising demand. Scalability guarantees that the system won't encounter major hiccups or malfunctions as workloads increase. This could entail employing cloud-based solutions, database sharding strategies, and microservices architecture when creating applications in software development. Scalability in business may entail adopting flexible operational methods, automating processes, and optimizing supply networks. Thanks to scalability, organizations can expand without being hindered by antiquated procedures or inadequate infrastructure.

Another benefit of automation is increased efficiency. Automating time-consuming and repetitive operations speeds up performance and lowers human error. Automation in software can be implemented through AI-driven optimizations, automated testing, and continuous integration and deployment (CI/CD). Workflow automation tools, robotic process automation (RPA), and customer relationship management (CRM) systems are examples of automation in business operations. Automation boosts productivity and frees up human resources to work on more important and innovative projects by reducing the need for manual intervention.

Enhancing data management procedures is another aspect of performance optimization. Decision-making relies heavily on data, and managing data inefficiently can result in errors and delays. Optimizing database queries, indexing, and caching frequently accessed data are all components of effective data management. It entails using big data analytics, ensuring appropriate data governance, and implementing data-driven decision-making techniques in corporate operations. Performance can be severely impacted by redundant procedures, inaccurate information, and resource waste brought on by poor data management. Successful data management optimization gives businesses a competitive edge by enabling them to make decisions more quickly and accurately.

Another crucial element in performance optimization is latency reduction. The term "latency" describes processing lags in network communications, software applications, and business workflows. Technologies like content delivery networks (CDNs), asynchronous processing, and effective algorithms can all help reduce latency. Reducing latency in business processes includes utilizing real-time collaboration tools, cutting down on bureaucracy, and optimizing communication channels. Quicker reaction times boost output, foster a more flexible workplace, and increase customer happiness.

Although it is frequently disregarded, security is a crucial component of speed improvement. A system susceptible to security risks may experience hiccups, lags, or fail. Performance is protected from security threats by using secure coding techniques, frequent vulnerability checks, and adherence to industry standards. Businesses can lower the risk of data breaches and system failures by implementing cybersecurity measures, including encryption, access controls, and employee training. In addition to being quick and effective, a well-optimized system is also resistant to attacks.

Maintaining great performance requires a culture of constant improvement. Optimization is a continuous process that necessitates creativity, flexibility, and a readiness to try out novel strategies. Companies may stay ahead of the curve by fostering a culture of learning and development. Regular training sessions, information exchange, and developing an efficient attitude facilitate long-term performance improvements. When optimization is embraced as a fundamental value, teams and employees are more likely to look for inefficiencies and develop solutions actively.

Performance improvement inherently involves balancing trade-offs. There are limitations in any system, and improving one component may come at the expense of another. For instance, boosting a software application's speed could require more memory, while cutting expenses in a company might affect quality. Finding the ideal balance that supports overarching goals is crucial. Cost, speed, scalability, and user experience are just a few variables that decision-makers must carefully weigh when evaluating trade-offs. Effective utilization of resources is ensured by prioritizing optimization activities according to their impact and viability.

In optimization, simplicity is essential. Overly complicated solutions frequently result in inefficiencies, higher maintenance expenses, and a greater chance of mistakes. Following modular design, clean coding standards, and simple architecture achieves better software development performance. Business efficiency is increased by optimizing workflows, eliminating pointless procedures, and concentrating on vital skills. The adage "less is more" is applicable in optimization since needless complexity frequently results in unforeseen performance problems.

Another crucial factor in optimization attempts is user experience. A system that works effectively but is hard to use eventually falls short of its goal. Performance optimization in software shouldn't come at the expense of usability. Smooth interactions, quick load times, and user-friendly interfaces enhance the user experience. Similarly, increasing efficiency in commercial operations shouldn't lead to impersonal or unduly strict procedures that irritate clients or staff—more sustainable and efficient optimization results from a well-rounded strategy that considers usability and performance.

Performance optimization is greatly impacted by cooperation and communication. In large-scale initiatives, inefficiencies frequently occur due to inadequate team coordination. Overall efficiency is increased by promoting open communication, utilizing collaborative technologies, and coordinating departmental goals. Adopting DevOps techniques in software development facilitates the integration of development and operations, resulting in improved system dependability and quicker deployments. Cross-functional cooperation guarantees that corporate-level optimization initiatives are comprehensive and not limited to discrete domains.

Sustainability and energy efficiency are becoming crucial factors in performance optimization. Long-term efficiency can be achieved by minimizing electronic waste, optimizing data center energy use, and implementing eco-friendly procedures. Companies may save money, comply with regulations, and improve their brand image by integrating sustainability into their optimization strategy. Sustainable optimization ensures that environmental effect is not sacrificed for efficiency advantages.

Using cutting-edge technologies improves performance optimization initiatives. Data analytics, machine learning, and artificial intelligence offer strong instruments for finding trends, anticipating inefficiencies, and automating decision-making. While predictive analytics in corporate operations improve forecasts and resource allocation, AI-driven optimizations in software applications increase speed and adaptability. Organizations can maintain their lead in performance optimization by embracing technology improvements.

Lastly, a crucial step in the optimization process is success measurement. Optimization efforts' evaluation is challenging without quantifiable objectives and unambiguous standards. Progress can be monitored through data-driven insights, realistic target setting, and the establishment of key performance indicators (KPIs). Measurable outcomes are the foundation of continuous improvement, which enables businesses to hone their tactics and guarantee long-term performance improvements.

Performance optimization is a complex field that necessitates a deliberate approach, ongoing development, and flexibility in response to shifting conditions. In any industry, including software development and corporate operations, performance optimization results in higher productivity, lower expenses, and better results. Organizations and individuals can attain optimal performance by recognizing bottlenecks, efficiently managing resources, utilizing automation, and embracing innovation. Optimization is a continuous process, and individuals who put it first have a competitive edge in a world that is becoming increasingly demanding.

CONCLUSION

Learning JavaScript Fast: Essential Coding Skills for Beginners: Build Web Interactivity Using Powerful JavaScript Tools. It can initially seem intimidating, but it can be a rewarding talent with time and constant practice. With the help of this book, you can now learn the principles of JavaScript, work with data, manipulate the Document Object Model (DOM), handle asynchronous operations, and even delve into more complex subjects like object-oriented and functional programming. You have developed a solid foundation in JavaScript by adhering to the ideas and methods covered, giving you the tools you need to create dynamic online apps.

You have learned how JavaScript functions and practical applications along this journey. You now know how to debug common mistakes, optimize efficiency, and develop clear, effective, and well-structured code. You can now create dynamic, user-friendly web experiences by delving into event management, asynchronous programming, and browser APIs. You are now well on your way to using the same tools that experienced developers use to construct contemporary web applications.

But there's more to knowing JavaScript than this. The language is still developing with new features, libraries, and frameworks appearing often. Continuously coding, exploring, and creating projects is the best way to keep getting better. The foundation you have established will be useful whether you choose to work with well-known JavaScript frameworks like React or Vue, create full-stack applications, or focus on front-end development.

As you progress, work with other developers, take on real-world projects, and experiment with more complex JavaScript ideas. Read the documentation, participate in coding communities, and keep up with market developments. You will become more competent and self-assured as you use what you have learned.

You now possess the necessary abilities to fully utilize the potential of JavaScript, one of the most potent and popular programming languages available today. You can create dynamic and captivating web applications from your ideas if you are persistent and creative. Continue studying and coding, and above all, relish becoming a proficient JavaScript developer.

Thank you for buying and reading/ listening to our book. If you found this book useful/ helpful please take a few minutes and leave a review on the platform where you purchased our book. Your feedback matters greatly to us.

www.ingramcontent.com/pod-product-compliance
Lightning Source LLC
LaVergne TN
LVHW022056200926
848481LV00003B/930
* 9 7 9 8 3 4 9 2 8 8 4 8 7 *